2000 SUPPLEMENT

to

MATERIALS ON

ACCOUNTING FOR LAWYERS

SECOND EDITION

by

DAVID R. HERWITZ
Austin Wakeman Scott Professor of Law
Harvard University Law School

MATTHEW J. BARRETT
Associate Professor of Law
Notre Dame Law School

UNIVERSITY CASEBOOK SERIES

Foundation Press
2000

 *TEXT IS PRINTED ON 10% POST CONSUMER RECYCLED PAPER*

PREFACE TO THE 2000 SUPPLEMENT

Thank you for selecting and using our materials. In our effort to provide the most timely, accurate and helpful materials possible, we want to highlight developments occurring since the second edition went to press and to call to your attention a number of typos, substantive errors and other glitches that appear in the casebook. We also want to apologize for any inconvenience that these mistakes may cause and to assure you that we will make every effort to prevent such errors from appearing in the next edition.

This 2000 Supplement, therefore, lists various errata in this preface and then proceeds to cover developments occurring between December 31, 1996, the cut-off date for the second edition, and April 30, 2000, plus selected "subsequent events" primarily involving international accounting principles and auditor independence. The discussion in this supplement parallels the casebook, including cross references to chapter headings and page numbers. As to the supplemental materials, the authors gratefully acknowledge invaluable help from Debbie Sumption in preparing the manuscript and the superb research assistance of Benjamin Jilek, Brian Neach, Janet Pollock and Gabriel Tsui, Notre Dame law students in the Classes of 2002, 2001, 2002 and 2000, respectively. The 1999 Form 10-K for Ben & Jerry's Homemade, Inc. has been reprinted with permission.

Below we list potentially misleading typographic errors and omissions. Please note that we have not included every typo in the list that follows. For example, we know that on page 123, second paragraph, second line: the word "refer" should be "refers." As another example, on page 244, in the third to the last line of the first paragraph, the word "selects" should be "select." The casebook also contains numerous formatting errors, especially in the first chapter, and assorted other glitches, including missing periods or commas, that we do not think can mislead anyone or create any substantive confusion. We apologize again. We hope that you will call any other errors or omissions to our attention.

Page 22, Problem 1.1A(2): insert the word "sheet" after the words "simple balance" at the end of the line

Page 30, Proprietorship T-account: missing a line down the middle to separate debit from credits

Page 32, Cash T-account: the amount for entry (4) should be "230" rather than "250"

Page 33, Proprietorship T-account: the $950, 525 and $1,475 amounts and related descriptions should be on the credit side, rather than the debit side, of the account

Page 53, second full paragraph, second line: the third and fourth words should be "capital surplus" rather than "stated capital"

Page 53, two lines above the last journal entry on the page: the word "share" should be "shares"

Page 83, last journal entry: both amounts should be "$120" rather than "$60"

Page 84, first journal entry: Deferred Salary Expense (as a debit) should appear directly under Salary Expense rather than be indented

Page 85, Accounts Payable: Robertson T-account: should not show a double underline, but should show a zero balance at the end of the period

Page 85, Accounts Payable: Ryan T-account: should show a single line under the July 13 entry

Page 85, Telephone Expense T-account: the "$25 (f)" should be in the credit column

Page 86, Land T-account: the vertical line should be to the right rather than to the left of the $1,800

Page 86, Deferred Salary Expense T-account: the vertical line should be to the right of the $180 and $120, but to the left of the $60

Page 86, Professional Income T-account: on the debit side, delete the "7-13 $100"

Page 87, the July 31 balance sheet for E. Tutt: the amount for Deferred Income in the Liabilities section should be "$200" rather than "$300"

Page 87, immediately before the Balance Sheet at the bottom of the page: ignore the statement in the last sentence of the text that the blank financial statement forms show the correct net income figure and balance sheet totals because the blank forms do not show these totals

Page 96, runover paragraph at the bottom, sixth line, near end: the word "debiting" should be "crediting"

Page 96, runover paragraph at the bottom, last line: the word "Debiting" should be "Crediting"

Page 103, balance sheet for Nifty Novelty Company: delete the reference to "Income Receivable" on the asset side

Page 103, balance sheet for Nifty Novelty Company: the heading for the right side of the balance sheet should be "Liabilities and Partners' Equity"

Page 110, last line: Net Cash Provided by Operating Activities should be "[$] 3,903,410"

Page 166, third full paragraph, second line: the first word should be "auditing" rather than "accounting"

Page 226, last line before the "chart" at the bottom of the page: "1.83846" should be "1.22504"

Page 238, second line: "four" should be "fourth"

Page 240, first full paragraph, ninth line: "$925.83" should be "$925.93"

Page 244, first paragraph, eighth and eleventh lines: replace "(b)" with "(c)" and "(c)" with "(b)" and switch the order of those sentences so that the revised "(b)" precedes the revised "(c)"

Page 274, first word: replace the word "sales" with "average assets"

Page 287, fourth line: insert "as" between "requirements" and "Management's"

Page 318, first line after the "(ii) Earned Surplus and Probably Capital Surplus" heading: "statutes" should be "states"

Page 342, second full paragraph, third line: "they" should be "there"

Page 359, first paragraph after "Conclusion and Summary" heading, sixth line: "many" should be "may"

Page 392, first full paragraph, end of third line: "Value" should be "Valley"

Page 393, last line before subsection (iii): the credit entry should read "Profit on Land Sale under Cost Recovery Method"

Page 409, second line: replace the words "interest market" at the end of the line with "market interest rate"

Page 409, middle of the page: "$82.19 amortized discount" should be "$82.19 amortized premium"

Page 417, right side of the T-account on the top of the page: Retained Earnings should be "175,000" rather than "225,000"

Page 430, in the Interest Computation column in the chart at the top of the page, the fractions for Years 3, 4 and 5 should be "3/15", "2/15" and "1/15", respectively, rather than all shown as "4/15"

Page 440, second to the last line: "you" should be "your"

Page 442, third and fourth lines of the last sentence of paragraph 26 of APB Opinion No. 29 at the bottom of the page: delete the erroneously inserted phrase "the recorded amount of the nonmonetary asset received in exchange is determinable within reasonable limits,"

Page 479, Problem 6.8: The reference to Problem 6.6 in the first line should be to Problem 6.4

Page 484, beginning of first line: "ment" should be "ment's"

Page 484, second line: delete the second "the" before "an"

Page 497, Problem 6.11B(2), second line, first word: "for" should be "with"

Page 536, beginning of the sixth paragraph: "X's" should be "Scary Air's"

Page 592: eliminate the blank lines under "Total cost" and "$173,000" in the computation of weighted average cost near the top of the page

Page 593, second paragraph under the "d) Last-In, First-Out" heading, fourth line: the first "the" should be "them"

Page 600, first full paragraph, second to the last line: the second "of" should be "or"

Page 613, first full paragraph, sixteenth line: the second "of" should be "or"

Page 614, first word in the third line from the bottom: "or" should be "of"

Page 621, Problem 8.2C, end of the second line following the listing of purchases: the last word should be "quarter" rather than "year "

Page 630, fourth line under the paragraph that begins with "2." at the top of the page: "neither" should be "does"

Page 649, end of fourth line from the bottom: insert the word "and" before the word "to" at the end of the line Page 663, middle of page: both the debit and the credit should be in the amount of $62,500

Page 661, Problems 9.2B and 9.2C both assume no salvage value

Page 663, second journal entry on the page: the amounts for both Depreciation Expense and Accumulated Depreciation should be "$62,500" rather than "$32,500"

Page 669, last line of the chart: the word "amortized" should be "amortize"

Page 697, second to the last line of Problem 9.5A: "should" should be "may"

Page 698, end of seventh line: "this" should be "these"

Page 699, line 22: "forth" should be "fourth"

Page 701, middle of the page: the $58,247 amount for "Obligations Under Capital Leases (Current)" should be shown in the credit column

Page 703, Problem 9.7A, first line: replace the word "an" with "a noncancellable" (this problem also assumes that the Loebl Corporation's incremental borrowing rate equals or exceeds twelve percent annual interest)

    If you find any other problem that does not appear below, please let us know. You can reach Matt Barrett at <Matthew.J.Barrett.1@nd.edu>, by calling him at (219) 631-8121, or via fax at (219) 631-4197. You will not offend us in any way because we want our materials to be as accurate and helpful as possible. We also welcome any other comments or suggestions that you might be willing to share. Thanks again.

David R. Herwitz
Matthew J. Barrett

June 2000

TABLE OF CONTENTS

TABLE OF CASES

Principal cases are in **bold** type. Non-principal cases are in roman type. References are to Pages.

CHAPTER I

INTRODUCTION TO FINANCIAL STATEMENTS, BOOKKEEPING AND ACCRUAL ACCOUNTING

F. ACCRUAL ACCOUNTING

1. INTRODUCTION

b. BASIC PRINCIPLES

Page 61. Insert the following section:

(7) An Emerging Fair Value or Relevance Principle

As the text at least implies, financial statements based solely on historical costs typically do not provide the most relevant or helpful information for decision-making purposes. Increasingly, financial accounting requires enterprises to use fair value or market value, rather than historical cost, to report certain assets and liabilities. As a result, current financial accounting technically uses a so-called "mixed-attribute" system that combines historical cost-reporting with a fair value model. In a recent article, Professor Stanley Siegel notes this development and predicts that the "accounting principles of the twenty-first century may bear little resemblance to their forbears." In addition to replacing the historical cost principle, the movement to fair value also calls into question the objectivity, revenue recognition, consistency and full disclosure principles. Stanley Siegel, *The Coming Revolution in Accounting: The Emergence of Fair Value as the Fundamental Principle of GAAP*, 42 Wayne L. Rev. 1839, 1841, 1847-49, 1859 (1996).

In December 1999, the leading body of accounting rule makers in the United States published a document setting forth its preliminary views on measuring and reporting certain financial assets and liabilities at fair value. This document, which invited public comments through May 31, 2000, could mark an important step in a potential move toward accounting principles and rules that could eventually require enterprises to use fair value for all financial assets and liabilities. Financial Accounting Standards Board, Preliminary Views on major issues related to Reporting Financial Instruments and Certain Related Assets and Liabilities at Fair Value (Dec. 14, 1999).

In their preliminary views, the rule makers specifically stated that because they have not resolved all the conceptual and practical issues related to determining the fair values of financial assets and liabilities, they have not decided when, if ever, the basic financial statements should report such fair values. As possible alternatives, the rule makers note that they could require enhanced disclosures about fair values or a separate set of financial statements based upon fair value. Because market prices do not exist for many financial assets, enterprises would need to develop valuation models to determine fair value. Such valuation models would inherently depend upon subjective assumptions. Not surprisingly, various organizations of enterprises that must prepare financial statements, most notably the American Bankers Association, have questioned whether a move to fair value accounting would offer either relevance or reliability. In any event, such a significant change to the principles underlying financial accounting will almost certainly require several years to complete and implement.

CHAPTER II

THE DEVELOPMENT OF ACCOUNTING PRINCIPLES AND AUDITING STANDARDS

C. GENERALLY ACCEPTED ACCOUNTING PRINCIPLES

1. THE ESTABLISHMENT OF ACCOUNTING PRINCIPLES

Page 128. At the end of the second sentence, insert the following:

Under the leadership of current Chairman Arthur Levitt, who has shown significant interest in accounting issues, the SEC has devoted considerable attention to accounting matters. In that regard, senior officials at the SEC frequently referred to 1999 as "The Year of the Accountant." *See, e.g.,* Remarks by Norman S. Johnson (Feb. 26, 1999), available at <http://www.sec.gov/news/speeches/spch256.htm>; *see also* Lisa Fried, *Agency Also Targets Accounting Practices*, N.Y.L.J., Mar. 4, 1999, at 5; Rachel Witmer, *SEC to Work with FASB, EITF in 1999 To Guard Integrity of Accounting Principles*, 30 Sec. Reg. & L. Rep. (BNA) 1202 (1998) ("You heard it here first. 1999 may have to be the year of accounting.") (quoting Brian Lane, then Director, SEC Division of Corporation Finance). In recent years, the SEC has focused increasing time on financial frauds, financial reporting and disclosure, international accounting standards, and the quality of financial statements. In the months ahead, the SEC will likely lead the movement to global accounting standards.

a. SECURITIES AND EXCHANGE COMMISSION

Page 130. At the end of the citation near the bottom of the page for the runover block quote, insert the following:

From time to time, the SEC has recommended individuals for membership on the FASB and consulted in the appointment process. Especially during the recent selection of Edmund Jenkins as the FASB's chairman in 1997, SEC Chairman Arthur Levitt provided names of potential candidates, was kept informed throughout the process, and effectively cleared Jenkins' appointment. Steve Burkholder, *Retired Andersen Partner Edmund Jenkins Succeeds Beresford as Chairman of FASB*, 29 Sec. Reg. & L. Rep. (BNA) 903 (1997).

Page 131. After the citation to 17 C.F.R. § 210 (1996) at the end of the eleventh line from the bottom of the page, insert the following:

SEC officials have announced that the Commission will use amendments to Regulation S-X as a mechanism to attempt to protect the integrity of accounting standards in the United States. Rachel Witmer, *SEC to Work with FASB, EITF in 1999 To Guard Integrity of Accounting Principles*, 30 Sec. Reg. & L. Rep. (BNA) 1202 (1998).

Page 132. Replace the second to last sentence in the second paragraph with the following:

As of April 30, 2000, the SEC had issued fifty-four FRRs.

Page 132. Replace the last sentence in the third paragraph with the following:

During 1999, the SEC issued 120 AAERs. As of April 30, 2000, the SEC had published 1,249 AAERs.

Page 132. Replace the second sentence in the fourth paragraph and related citation with the following:

During fiscal 1999, "the SEC brought approximately 526 [enforcement actions], with 'close to' 100 cases in the area of financial fraud." Neil Hare, *Fraudulent Financial Reporting Tops Enforcement Priority List, Walker Declares*, 31 Sec. Reg. & L. Rep. (BNA) 1528 (1999). The total number of actions brought in fiscal 1999 represents about a ten percent increase over recent years. About twenty percent of the enforcement actions have historically involved financial frauds. Michael Bologna, *Trends in SEC Enforcement Shown in Cases, Walker Says*, 31 Sec. Reg. & L. Rep. (BNA) 584 (1999).

Page 133. Replace the last sentence in the first full paragraph with the following:

As of April 30, 2000, the SEC's staff had issued 101 SABs.

In 1997, the Division of Corporation Finance began issuing Staff Legal Bulletins ("SLBs"). Like SABs, these legal bulletins represent the views of the Division's staff. Once again, however, the SEC has neither approved nor disapproved the SLBs, and they are not rules or interpretations of the Commission. As of April 30, 2000, the Division had issued nine SLBs.

In an effort to provide additional guidance, the staff of the Division of Corporation Finance posts and periodically updates several other sources of information about the statutes, rules and regulations that the Division administers, some of which involve accounting issues, on the SEC's web site at <http://www.sec.gov> under the "Current SEC Rulemaking" and "Other Commission Notices and Information" links. These other sources include "Current Issues and Rulemaking Projects of the Division of Corporation Finance" (dated April 13, 2000); "Current Accounting and Disclosure Issues in the Division of Corporation Finance" (dated January 21, 2000); and "Division of Corporation Finance: Frequently Requested Accounting and Financial Reporting Interpretations and Guidance" (dated May 1, 1999). Each of these outlines cautions that they do not necessarily reflect the views or policies of the SEC, the Commissioners, or other members of the staff. Finally, the Division also responds each year to thousands of telephone inquiries, which often pose accounting issues. The Division posts and supplements a manual of staff telephone interpretations that seeks to provide "general guidance," but warns that users should not rely on the responses as definitive.

b. THE PRIVATE SECTOR

Page 136. In the second full paragraph, update the salary and budget information as follows:

The chairman's salary now stands at $460,000 annually, while the other six FASB members earn $374,000 per year. In 1999, the FAF's total expenses exceeded $21 million. Contributions to FASB amounted to about $6.4 million in 1999, dropping $101,000 from almost $6.5 million in 1998. The decline in contributions continues a trend that began more than ten years ago. In 1999, contributions accounted for almost twenty-nine percent of FASB's revenues. More than fifty-seven percent of gross contributions during 1999 came from the public accounting profession. Interestingly, users of financial statements have historically donated only about one percent of total contributions. Various trustees have suggested that apparent disagreement with FASB's recent rule-making among executives in certain industries helps to explain the drop in contributions from preparers. At the end of 1999, the FAF held about $27.5 million of investments in a reserve fund, an amount sufficient to allow FASB to continue to operate for several years even if contributions completely evaporated. About $3.3 million in investment income from the reserve fund during 1999 offset an operating deficit that exceeded $1 million. 1999 marked the third consecutive year that the FAF incurred an operating deficit. The potential loss of revenues from print publications and increasing pressures to offer free, electronic access to FASB materials present potentially more serious financial problems. Financial Accounting Foundation, 1999 ANNUAL REPORT 23, 25, 26 (2000); Paul B. W. Miller, Rodney J. Redding, & Paul R. Bahnson, THE FASB[:] THE PEOPLE, THE PROCESS, AND THE POLITICS 38, 39 (4th ed. 1998); Steve Burkholder, *FAF Told Downward Trend In Contributions Continues*, 31 Sec. Reg. & L. Rep. (BNA) 191 (1999).

Page 138. At the end of the carryover paragraph at the top of the page, add the following:

In 1998, the FASB finally completed its six and one-half year project on derivatives, or financial contracts that base their value on some underlying asset, such as bonds or foreign currencies, by issuing FASB Statement No. 133. In discussing the state of FASB in its twenty-fifth year, Chairman Edmund Jenkins recently cited the Board's "due process" as one of its strengths, adding that the Board has been trying to improve its internal process and reduce the time on individual standard-setting projects. Steve Burkholder, *FASB in 'Very Good' State, Jenkins Says; Baker Bill Casts Shadow*, 30 Sec. Reg. & L. Rep. (BNA) 251 (1998).

Page 138. In the runover paragraph at the bottom of the page, incorporate the following:

Effective July 1, 1998, Coopers & Lybrand and Price Waterhouse, formerly two of the "Big Six" accounting firms, merged to create PricewaterhouseCoopers, the world's largest professional services firm and also the one with the longest name. The merger reduces the Big Six to the Big Five. Earlier in 1998, Ernst & Young and KPMG Peat Marwick canceled their proposed merger, which would have created an even larger firm than PricewaterhouseCoopers, after Japan and Canada joined the United States and the European Community and announced plans for "prolonged regulatory review" of the combination. *Merger of Coopers, PW Takes Effect*, 30 Sec. Reg. & L. Rep. (BNA) 1033 (1998); Rachel Witmer, *Johnson Acknowledges SEC May Have Erred In Not Telling Auditors to Stick to Auditing*, 30 Sec. Reg. & L. Rep. (BNA) 386 (1998).

c. CONGRESS

Page 141. At the end of the carryover paragraph at the top of the page, insert the following paragraph:

The recent controversy over accounting for derivatives again illustrates the increased politicization of FASB matters and the growing tendency for disappointed special interests to seek recourse in Congress. During the standard setting process, bankers and derivatives dealers, in particular, voiced loud opposition to the draft rules, which proposed to require enterprises to record the fair market value of derivatives as either assets or liabilities on their balance sheets and to report certain changes in value of those derivatives on their income statements, and lobbied Congress in an effort to stop those draft rules from becoming effective.

After a public hearing in March 1997, the Senate Banking Securities Subcommittee issued a report calling on FASB to re-expose the derivatives proposal. Shortly thereafter, and apparently at the prompting of major banks, the American Bankers Association and the International Swaps and Derivatives Association, at least eighteen members of the House of Representatives sent letters containing identical language to FASB urging it to re-expose or otherwise allow more time for public comment on a revised, but nevertheless still controversial, proposal on derivatives, a process that, in either event, would have extended the timetable for issuing final rules.

Late in 1997, Senator Lauch Faircloth (R-NC), then a member of the Senate Banking Securities Subcommittee and chairman of the Senate Banking Financial Institutions Subcommittee, introduced Senate Bill No. 1560, the proposed Accurate Accounting Standards Certification Act. The bill would preclude the derivatives rules from applying to financial institutions unless bank regulators certify to Congress that the new rules would accurately reflect bank earnings and would not adversely affect prudent risk management. In an effort to counter the legislation, the Financial Accounting Foundation ("FAF"), FASB's parent organization, registered with Congress, naming its representatives as lobbyists on financial and banking legislation.

In early 1998, Representative Richard Baker (R-La), chairman of the House Banking Capital Markets and Securities Subcommittee, introduced a second measure, H.R. 3165, the proposed Financial Accounting Fairness Act of 1998, which would explicitly require the SEC to review FASB standards and other private sector rules that affect public companies, effectively shifting the setting of financial accounting standards from FASB to the SEC. The legislation would also allow anyone "aggrieved" by an accounting standard to file suit challenging the rule in federal court.

Despite those bills, FASB issued FASB Statement No. 133, Accounting for Derivative Instruments and Hedge Accounting, a final statement on derivatives as planned. Even though both bills died in the 105th Congress, which ended in 1998, and Senator Faircloth lost his bid for reelection, opponents of various accounting standards and rulemaking projects continue to seek Congressional intervention.

During the 106th Congress, which began in January 1999, President Clinton signed the Gramm-Leach-Bliley Act, the financial services reform law that allows banks, securities firms, insurance companies and other financial services providers to affiliate. That legislation contains a provision that requires the SEC to "consult and coordinate comments with the appropriate Federal banking agency before taking any action or rendering any opinion" on how any insured banking institution should report loan loss reserves in its financial statements. Gramm-Leach-Bliley Act, Pub. L. No. 106-102, § 241(a), 113 Stat. 1338, 1407 (1999). Under the accrual method of accounting, financial institutions treat their estimates for any uncollectible amounts in their loan portfolios as expenses. In 1998, the SEC expressed concern that financial institutions have intentionally overstated these allowances for loan losses in good economic times to pad against potential losses during economic downturns and, at least in some circumstances, sought to reduce the amount of these allowances, sometimes also referred to as loan loss reserves. Banking regulators objected to the SEC's efforts and warned that such efforts could cause banks to ignore conservatism and to cut reserves for loan losses. In the controversy that followed, both the Senate Banking Committee and the House Banking Financial

Institutions Subcommittee held hearings on loan loss reserves in 1999. As a result of such hearings, House Banking Financial Institutions Subcommittee Chairwoman Marge Roukema (R-N.J.) offered the language that appears above as a floor amendment to the House version of the financial services reform legislation. After the House of Representatives approved the amendment 407-20, the Congressional conferees included the provision in the final legislation.

At least thru April 30, 2000, no legislation dealing primarily with the FASB's ability to establish accounting principles had been introduced in the 106th Congress. Technology companies, investment banking firms and connected trade organizations, however, have sought Congressional assistance to oppose at least two current FASB rulemaking efforts: (i) the FASB's proposed interpretation of APB No. 25 that would require enterprises to recognize more expenses related to stock options; and (ii) the tentative position to move away from a long-standing practice in merger accounting that these businesses generally favor. Presumably as a result, the Senate Banking Committee held hearings on proposed accounting rules for mergers and acquisitions in 2000. The House Commerce Subcommittee on Finance and Hazardous Material also held hearings on the proposed merger and acquisition rules. To date, however, those hearings have not produced any specific legislative proposals. Ronald Taylor, *Bliley Critical of FASB Proposal, Says U.S. Business Interests Could Suffer*, 32 Sec. Reg. & L. Rep. (BNA) 617 (2000); Martha A. Matthews, *Economics of FASB Bid to End Pooling Considered by Senate Panel*, 32 Sec. Reg. & L. Rep. (BNA) 347 (2000), Steve Burkholder, *Senators Disagree With FASB On Need for 'New Rules' on Stock Options*, 31 Sec. Reg. & L. Rep. (BNA) 893 (1999); Steve Burkholder, *Tech Firms Prepare for Debate With FASB On Stock Options*, 31 Sec. Reg. & L. Rep. (BNA) 511 (1999).

d. INTERNATIONAL ACCOUNTING STANDARDS COMMITTEE

Pages 141-143. Replace the discussion with the following:

In today's global economy, investors, businesses and their lawyers need to understand local financial accounting and reporting practices. Different taxation systems, economic conditions, political processes and cultural traditions contribute to a diversity in accounting practices between nations in matters such as inventory valuation, depreciation, consolidations, and disclosure requirements. While serving as the chairman of the SEC in the early 1990s, Richard C. Breeden estimated that about eighteen percent of foreign companies would report more income on financial reports under U.S. standards than they did under their own countries' standards. In contrast, about thirty-three percent would report less under U.S. standards. Although these variations often occur on a country-by-country basis, they can differ from company-to-company in a particular country. Barbara Kirchheimer, *SEC Chief Accountant Offers New Definition Of 'Asset,'* Tax Notes, Jan. 18, 1993, at 338, 339.

To illustrate further, as we saw in Chapter I, the accounting standards in the United States generally follow the historical cost principle to value assets. In many foreign countries, particularly nations experiencing high inflationary rates, businesses use current values to record their assets. As another example, German and Japanese businesses have traditionally turned to banks rather than the equity markets for financing. Accordingly, the needs of creditors, rather than investors, have disproportionately influenced the financial reporting in those two countries relative to the United States.

The international business community needs and wants globally accepted accounting practices to facilitate the flow of capital between markets. Multinational enterprises around the world, especially in Germany, Switzerland and other European countries, increasingly seek to raise capital across borders and to list their securities on more than one stock market. These enterprises would prefer to use one set of accounting rules worldwide, so that they do not have to bear the burden and expense of reconciling financial statements prepared using their home country's accounting principles to generally accepted accounting principles in other jurisdictions. At the same time, the New York Stock Exchange and exchanges in Canada, Europe, London and Japan are clamoring for international accounting rules. So far, however, legislators and regulators in the United States, as well as in Tokyo and Toronto, have not endorsed international accounting standards. Nevertheless, harmonization of accounting standards in the very near future seems inevitable. Lawyers and their clients should pay careful attention to this important topic.

Very early in the twenty-first century, the world will likely see the leading economic nations adopt international accounting standards. Dating back to 1995, bodies of the International Accounting Standards Committee ("IASC") and the International Organization of Securities Commissions "IOSCO") agreed to develop and endorse international accounting standards before the end of the twentieth century so that businessess could raise capital across borders. In March 1999, IASC issued new rules on financial instruments, including derivatives, that completed the set of core standards for global accounting principles that IASC subsequently submitted to IOSCO for possible use in cross-border securities offerings. On May 17, 2000, IOSCO announced that the organization has recommended that its members allow multinational issuers to use thirty IASC standards, as enhanced by supplemental treatments where necessary to address outstanding substantive issues at a national or regional level. These supplement treatments could include reconciliation, additional disclosure, and interpretation by specifying a particular accounting alternative or treatment when permissible options or uncertainty exist.

IASC's history dates back to 1973, when an agreement among professional accountancy bodies from Australia, Canada, France, Germany, Japan, Mexico, the Netherlands, the United Kingdom and Ireland, and the United States established the organization. Beginning in 1983 and lasting until May 2000 amendments to IASC's constitution become effective, likely late in 2000 or early in 2001 when a self-perpetuating board of nineteen trustees assumes control of the organization, IASC's members included every professional accountancy body that belongs to the International Federation of Accountants ("IFAC"). In June 2000, the "About IASC" link off IASC's home page on the World Wide Web at <http://www.iasc.org.uk> reported that membership in IASC included 143 professional accountancy organizations from 104 countries, plus sixteen associate or affiliate members.

As of April 30, 2000, IASC, through its Board, had issued thirty-nine International Accounting Standards ("IASs"). IASs, however, do not establish principles that AICPA members must follow under the Institute's Code of Professional Conduct. American Institute of Certified Public Accountants, 2 Professional Standards (CCH) AC § 9000 Introduction, at 11,002 (Aug. 1999). In fact, following IASs will often violate U.S. GAAP. In that regard, FASB recently published a 502 page report that both identifies numerous variations that existed between GAAP in the United States and IASC standards and analyzes those differences. Financial Accounting Standards Board, THE IASC-U.S. COMPARISON PROJECT: A REPORT ON THE SIMILARITIES AND DIFFERENCES BETWEEN IASC STANDARDS AND U.S. GAAP (Carrie Bloomer, ed., 2d ed. 1999). Although many of the variations between U.S. GAAP and IASC standards do not qualify as major, and on-going developments will continue to eliminate or reduce deviations, significant differences in recognition and measurement standards, the presence of choices or alternatives in both U.S. and IASC accounting principles, and lack of specific guidance in certain areas continue to exist. At the same time, the almost certain likelihood that the industrialized world will soon embrace some system of global accounting standards warrants serious consideration, especially when drafting and negotiating agreements involving enterprises interested in cross-border securities listings.

On May 24, 2000, IASC's members, the professional accountancy bodies in more than 100 countries, adopted a new constitution that restructures IASC into an independent foundation that parallels FAF, only on an international level. Under the restructuring, IASC's governance shall rest with two main bodies, the Trustees and the Board. The new constitution, however, also describes both a Standards Interpretation Committee and a Standards Advisory Council.

The Trustees will include nineteen individuals, selected pursuant to a formula designed to ensure geographic diversity. Another formula seeks to maintain a balance of professional backgrounds, including individuals from prominent international accounting firms, organizations that prepare and use financial statements, and the academy. The Trustees, who, after an initial transition period, serve staggered, three-year terms will select subsequent trustees, appoint members to the IASC Board, raise the estimated $16 million needed each year to fund the organization's operations, and exercise general oversight over the foundation's operations. Shortly before IASC's members adopted the new constitution, a separate Nominating Committee that SEC Chairman Arthur Levitt headed, selected the initial Trustees. Paul A. Volcker, Former Chairman, U.S. Federal Reserve Board, agreed to serve as the first chair of the Trustees.

IASC's Board will hold sole responsibility for setting accounting standards. In an important change from IASC's previous structure, the fourteen person board will include twelve full-time individuals, who must sever all employment relationships with their current employers and shall not hold any position giving rise to economic incentives that might call into question their independence of judgment in setting accounting standards, and two part-time members, who need not commit all their time to paid employment with IASC. In an effort to balance perspectives and experience, the new constitution requires the Trustees to appoint at least five members from public accounting, three individuals from industry, three persons from the investment community, and one member from the academy. The Trustees will tap members for their expertise rather than their national or regional identification. Under the "old" IASC Board, only organizations, and not individuals, could serve as members. Unlike FASB, the "old" IASC Board operated as a part-time and volunteer group, which generally held one week meetings, four times a year, with a small staff and meager budget. Until 1999, the "old" IASC Board's operating procedures did not open its meetings to the public. Although the new constitution allows the IASC Board to meet in private to consider selection, appointment and other personnel issues, the Board will generally meet in public at such times and locations as the Board determines.

For each project, the Board must publish an exposure draft for public comment and consider any comments before issuing final International Accounting Standards. Under the new constitution, eight of the fourteen members of the Board must approve the publication of an exposure draft or a final International Accounting Standard.

The new constitution empowers the Standing Interpretations Committee ("SIC"), a twelve-member panel that will meet as and when required and whose members serve three-year terms, to decide "contentious" accounting issues arising from the application of IASs. In essence, SIC will perform the same function for IASC as the Emerging Issues Task Force ("EITF") does for FASB. In this role, SIC shall interpret IASs, publish draft interpretations for public comment, consider timely comments before finalizing an interpretation, and obtain IASC Board approval for final interpretations. If no more than three members of the panel vote against an interpretation, SIC will ask the IASC Board to issue the interpretation. Eight of the fourteen members of the Board must approve the publication of a final interpretation. Under the predecessor constitution, three-quarters of the IASC Board needed to approve an interpretation for final publication. Under those rules, the "old" IASC Board had approved sixteen interpretations for fiscal periods beginning on or before April 30, 2000, and a seventeenth interpretation that applies only to fiscal periods beginning on or after July 1, 2000. Presumably, IASC will continue to number final interpretations sequentially, such as SIC-1 and SIC-2.

The Standards Advisory Council ("SAC") will give advice to the IASC Board on agenda decisions and priorities for the Board's work, inform the Board on their views on major rulemaking projects, and otherwise advise the Trustees and Board, especially on any proposed changes to the new constitution. The Trustees will appoint about thirty individuals with diverse geographic and functional backgrounds and an interest in international financial reporting to renewable, three-year terms on SAC.

As IASC restructures and IASs garner increased international acceptance, pressure continues to build on the SEC to permit both foreign and domestic registrants to follow IASs. In recent years, the SEC, which belongs to the IOSCO, has eased the burden on foreign registrants by accepting financial statements that comply with several IASs. For example, the SEC already allows foreign registrants to present financial statements in any currency that the registrant deems appropriate for the U.S. market and to prepare cash flow statements in accordance with IAS No. 7, "Cash Flow Statements." In general, however, the SEC has resisted relaxing its rules, which almost certainly rank as the toughest in the world, to allow foreign registrants to sell securities in the United States. Donald Schwartz, *The Future of Financial Accounting: Universal Standards*, J. ACCT., May 1996, at 20; *SEC Adopts Rules to Reduce Paperwork for U.S., Foreign Registrants*, 26 Sec. Reg. & L. Rep. (BNA) 1679 (1994); Suzanne E. Rothwell, *When companies over there want to sell securities over here*, BUS. L. TODAY, July/Aug. 1993, at 32; *see also* M. Elizabeth Rader, *Accounting Issues in Cross-Border Securities Offerings*, 17 FORDHAM INT'L L. J. S129 (1994).

The National Securities Markets Improvement Act of 1996 expressed the sense of Congress that "the establishment of a high-quality comprehensive set of generally accepted international accounting standards in cross-border securities offerings would greatly facilitate international financing activities." The legislation further encouraged the SEC to "enhance its vigorous support for the development of high-quality international accounting standards as soon as practicable." Finally, the law directed the Commission to report to Congress within one year on the efforts to develop, and the outlook for successful completion of, a core set of international accounting standards that the SEC would accept. Pub. L. No. 104-290, § 509, 110 Stat. 3416, 3449-50; *see also SEC Must Report On Writing Of Core International Accounting Standards*, 28 Sec. Reg. & L. Rep. (BNA) 1360 (1996).

In October 1997, and pursuant to the legislative directive in the National Securities Markets Improvement Act of 1996, the SEC submitted its report, interestingly entitled "Report on Promoting Global Preeminence of American Securities Markets" to Congress. The document states that IASC's efforts have already contributed significantly to raising the quality of accounting standards worldwide and reducing the differences between international accounting standards and U.S. accounting principles. Nevertheless, the report emphasized that "[a]t this point, it is not clear what the Commission's final decision regarding the core standards project will be." Securities & Exchange Commission, Report on Promoting Global Preeminence of American Securities Markets (Oct. 1997) (available at <http://www.sec.gov/news/studies/acctgsp.htm>).

Until IASC announced plans to amend its constitution to allow an independent body, seemingly free from commercial interests, to issue IASs, many commentators, including members of FASB and the SEC's staff, expressed serious doubts about the chances that the SEC would ultimately endorse the core standards, especially without reconciliation to U.S. GAAP or additional disclosures. Some critics even referred to the core standards as "IASC lite" or "FASB Lite." Shortly after IASC announced the proposed structure for its new constitution, SEC Chief Accountant Lynn Turner and FASB Chairman Edmund Jenkins expressed support for the IASC plan. SEC Chairman Arthur Levitt's willing to chair the special nominating committee to select the restructured IASC's first trustees seemingly bodes well for the core standards. *See Accounting Briefs*, 32 Sec. Reg. & L. Rep. (BNA) 268 (2000); Steve Burkholder, IASC Resolves to Change Structure; FASB Backs Change '100 Percent,' 31 Sec. Reg. & L. Rep. (BNA) 1554, 1555 (1999).

Under the Administrative Procedure Act, the SEC must give formal notice and allow a period for public comment before adopting international accounting principles. In early 2000, the SEC issued a concept release that identified the following five essential elements to a high quality financial reporting infrastructure: effective, independent and high quality accounting and auditing standard setters; high quality auditing standards, audit firms with effective quality controls worldwide; profession-wide quality assurance; and active regulatory oversight. By posing twenty-six different questions, the concept release requested comments as to whether the IASC core standards satisfy the following three broad criteria that the SEC set forth in a 1996 statement for evaluating those core standards:

(1) Do the IASC standards constitute a comprehensive, generally accepted basis of accounting?

(2) Do the standards must qualify as "high quality" in that they provide transparency, comparability and full disclosure?

(3) Will rigorous interpretation and enforcement accompany the standards?

The comment period ended on May 23, 2000. Concept Release on International Accounting Standards, 65 Fed. Reg. 8896 (2000).

As part of FASB's international efforts, the organization has been working with other national standard setters on various harmonization projects. Most notably, and as a member of the so-called "G4 +1" group, FASB has published discussion papers on various accounting topics. The "G4 + 1" actually includes representatives from six accounting rulemaking bodies--FASB, its counterparts in Australia, Canada, New Zealand and the United Kingdom, plus observers from IASC. As another example, FASB and IASC collaborated before issuing FASB Statement No. 128 and IAS No. 33, both entitled "Earnings per Share," at almost the same time in 1997. Although FASB Statement No. 128 requires additional footnote disclosures, the two pronouncements collectively represent the first international standard on that subject. More recently, FASB worked with both the Canadian Institute of Chartered Accountants and IASC on FASB Statement No. 131, Disclosures about Segments of an Enterprise and Related Information. As the FASB moves away from historical cost reporting of financial assets and liabilities for example, the Board has also been working with IASC on a fair value project. After recently completing its controversial project on derivatives, the FASB reportedly now devotes more time to international accounting standards than to any other issue.

As the movement toward harmonization continues, leaders in the accounting community in the United States have speculated about the FASB's decline or even demise. Both SEC Chairman Arthur Levitt and Chief Accountant Lynn Turner have predicted that the FASB will continue to assume an important role in standard-setting. Even with global accounting standards, a two-tier reporting system in the

United States remains a definite possibility. Under that scenario, multinational firms would use international accounting standards, while the SEC would continue to require domestic companies to apply U.S. GAAP. Critics, however, complain that such a scenario would create an unlevel playing field in accounting. *See generally* James D. Cox, *Regulatory Duopoly in U.S. Securities Markets*, 99 Colum. L. Rev. 1200, 1202, 1214 n.7 (1999) (concluding that the SEC should continue to promote convergence between IASs and U.S. GAAP and opining that whether to limit IASs to foreign issuers or to permit domestic firms to use IASs to satisfy SEC reporting requirements poses the biggest political issue).

4. CRITIQUE

Page 153. After the first full paragraph, insert the following:

Borrowing from repeated references by top SEC officials to 1999 as the "Year of the Accountant," some pundits have referred to 2000 as the "Year of the Audit Committee." Beginning in late 1998, SEC Chairman Arthur Levitt repeatedly expressed concerns about the adequacy of audit committees' oversight of the financial reporting process after accounting irregularities arose at various companies, including Cendant Corp., Livent Inc. and Sunbeam Corp. The failures of audit committees to monitor financial reporting effectively contributed to many of these frauds. *See, e.g.*, Jeffrey Goldfarb, *Broadway Musical Producers Face SEC, Criminal Accounting Fraud Charges*, 31 Sec. Reg. & L. Rep. (BNA) 77, 78 (1999); Joann S. Lublin and Elizabeth MacDonald, *Management: Scandals Signal Laxity of Audit Panels*, Wall St. J., July 17, 1998, at B1. Criticizing the make-up and amount of time audit committees actually spend reviewing financial reports, Levitt noted that audit committees at some companies have included trios such as: (i) a professor, a politician and an engineer; (ii) a former Marine officer, the head of a nonprofit and a former politician; and (iii) a school instructor, a Veterans Administration nurse and a nonprofit executive. Levitt continued: "There's nothing wrong with those professions, but an audit committee must really represent the watchdog of what goes on in a corporation." Jeffrey Goldfarb, *New Panel to Devise Stricter Oversight Proposals for Independent Auditors*, 30 Sec. Reg. & L. Rep. (BNA) 1455 (1998).

In an effort to address Chairman Levitt's concerns, the New York Stock Exchange ("NYSE") and National Association of Securities Dealers ("NASD") immediately created a blue ribbon panel to offer recommendations on strengthening the role of audit committees. In February 1999, the panel issued its report which, among other things, called on the NYSE and NASD to take actions designed to enhance the independence of audit committees and to strengthen their effectiveness. The report also asked the SEC to propose rules requiring written charters for, certain procedures by and disclosures from, audit committees. REPORT AND RECOMMENDATIONS OF THE BLUE RIBBON COMMITTEE ON IMPROVING THE EFFECTIVENESS OF CORPORATE AUDIT COMMITTEES (1999), *reprinted at* 54 Bus. Law. 1067; see also National Association of Corporate Directors, REPORT OF THE NACD BLUE RIBBON COMMISSION ON AUDIT COMMITTEES: A PRACTICAL GUIDE (2000) (containing sample audit committee charter, questions for audit committees, and audit committee calendar).

In response to the panel's report, NASD, NYSE and ASE proposed, and the SEC approved, changes to their listing standards. Most significantly, these changes give the audit committee the right to hire and terminate the auditor. These changes also require audit committees to include at least three members, limit membership to "independent" and "financially literate" directors, mandate that at least one member possess accounting or financial management expertise, and more rigorously define "independent." In December 1999 the SEC issued final rules that require registrants to include certain information in their proxy statements: a report from their audit committee, disclosures regarding the independence of the audit committee members, and a copy of the audit committee's charter at least once every three years. In particular, the audit committee's report requires a statement whether the audit committee recommended to the board of directors that the registrant include the audited financial statements for the last fiscal year in the annual report that enterprises must file with the Commission on either Form 10-K or, for small business issuers, Form 10-KSB. The new rules and amendments apply to all proxy statements relating to votes occurring after December 15, 2000. Audit Committee Disclosure, 64 Fed. Reg. 73,389 (1999) (to be codified at 17 C.F.R. §§ 228.306, 229.306); Phyllis Diamond, *Audit Committees Will Face Greater Scrutiny Under SEC Rule Changes*, 31 Sec. Reg. & L. Rep. (BNA) 1664, 1665 (1999).

Page 153. After the citation to the Public Oversight Board's 1994-95 Annual Report in the last paragraph near the bottom of the page, insert the following:

After exhortations from SEC Chairman Arthur Levitt and a recommendation from the Blue Ribbon Committee on Improving the Effectiveness of Corporate Audit Committees, the AICPA's Auditing Standards Board issued a new SAS that requires an auditor to discuss certain information relating to the auditor's judgments about the quality, not just the acceptability, of the enterprise's accounting principles with the audit committees of SEC registrants. The new rules apply to audits for periods ending on or after December 15, 2000. Statement of Auditing Standards No. 90, Audit Committee Communications (American Inst. of Certified Pub. Accountants 1999).

D. GENERALLY ACCEPTED AUDITING STANDARDS

Page 155. Replace the last sentence of the third paragraph with the following:

As a result, the accounting profession, through the AICPA's Auditing Standards Board and via the profession's participation on the newly established Independence Standards Board, which the SEC and the AICPA created in 1997, more frequently influences and determines "generally accepted auditing standards" or "GAAS."

1. THE INDEPENDENT AUDITOR'S ROLE

a. INDEPENDENCE

Pages 156-158. Replace the discussion for this section with the following:

As this chapter has already suggested, independence serves as the cornerstone for the auditing profession. All lawyers should understand the distinct role that auditors play and appreciate the difference between the responsibilities of an auditor and an attorney. Basically, lawyers act as advocates, while auditors serve as independent attestators, for their clients. In essence, an auditor must treat the financial markets, rather than the enterprise undergoing the audit or its management, as the real client. In the words of Professor Calvin H. Johnson, "[Auditors] owe no duty to the firm: In the game of auditing, the accountants are the cops and managers are the robbers." Calvin H. Johnson, *Accounting in Favor of Investors*, 19 Cardozo L. Rev. 637, 638 (1997).

In United States v. Arthur Young & Co., 465 U.S. 805, 104 S.Ct. 1495, 79 L.Ed.3d 826 (1984), the Supreme Court contrasted the roles of attorneys and independent auditors in holding that an auditor must disclose audit workpapers in response to a subpoena that the Internal Revenue Service had issued. As we already know, attorneys serve as confidential advisors and advocates for clients. The lawyer's duty of loyalty requires a lawyer to present the client's case in the most favorable possible light. In contrast, an auditor assumes a different role which the Supreme Court described as "a disinterested analyst charged with public obligations." The Supreme Court wrote:

> By certifying the public reports that collectively depict a corporation's financial status, the independent auditor assumes a public responsibility transcending any employment relationship with the client. The independent public accountant performing this special function owes ultimate allegiance to the corporation's creditors and stockholders, as well as to investing public. This "public watchdog" function demands that the accountant maintain total independence from the client at all times and requires complete fidelity to the public trust.

465 U.S. at 817-18, 104 S.Ct. at 1503, 79 L.Ed.2d at 835-37. *But see* Daniel R. Fischel, *Lawyers and Confidentiality*, 65 U. Chi. L. Rev. 1, 19-21, 33 (1998)

(disagreeing with the Supreme Court's distinction between the roles of attorneys and independent auditors; arguing that, as reputational intermediaries, lawyers and auditors perform far more similar economic functions than the Court's analysis suggests; and ultimately concluding that "[a]bsent some more compelling justification for [attorney confidentiality rules, such as the ethical duty of confidentiality, the attorney-client privilege, and the work product doctrine,] than has been advanced to date, these doctrines should be abolished").

To maintain the public's confidence in our system, an auditor must remain independent. To keep from violating SEC rules and professional standards, auditing firms, their owners and audit employees cannot own any direct financial interest or material indirect financial interest in an audit client, its parent, any subsidiaries or other affiliates. 17 C.F.R. § 210.2-01(b) (1999); *see also* In re Rider, Accounting and Auditing Enforcement Release No. 555, [1991-1995 Accounting and Auditing Enforcement Releases Transfer Binder] Fed. Sec. L. Rep. (CCH) ¶ 74,015 (1994) (permanently denying an auditor who owned 2,000 shares of common stock in an audit client the privilege of appearing or practicing before the SEC as an accountant). Independence, however, also requires both intellectual honesty and honesty in appearance. To qualify as honest in appearance, an auditor must avoid any circumstance which a reasonable person might consider likely to influence independence adversely. For example, the general public might question an auditor's independence if the auditor's spouse worked for the client even though the auditor exercised intellectual honesty during the audit.

The following speech by SEC Chairman Arthur Levitt both highlights the SEC's recent concerns regarding independence and sets forth an action plan to address the perceived problems:

"Renewing the Covenant With Investors," remarks by Arthur Levitt

Chairman, Securities and Exchange Commission
New York University, Center for Law and Business, May 10, 2000
(available at <http://www.sec.gov/news/speeches/spch370.txt>).

* * * Steady growth, low inflation, and record employment have cultivated fertile ground for America's companies. All the while, more Americans than ever before are investing in the stock market.

In times of great prosperity, however, it's easy to forget that investors commit capital because they have a basic confidence in the quality and integrity of America's markets. That faith does more than fuel markets – it makes markets possible. Nothing promotes and preserves this confidence more than a strong, transparent and accountable financial reporting framework.

More than eighteen months ago, * * * I expressed my concern that corporate America's motivation to meet Wall Street earnings expectations could be overriding common sense business practices. * * *

In the time since, I've been encouraged by how this issue has taken hold in the minds of business executives, corporate directors, investors, and the financial media alike. Through the concerted work of many in the financial community, we have made progress – enacting new rules for audit committees and refocusing on fundamental concepts in the accounting framework.

* * *

Make Your Numbers, or Else

Yet, as I reflect more on my conversations with corporate executives, accountants, analysts and others, as I read stories that continue to illuminate an element of game playing, it's become increasingly clear that the essence of our misgivings about the state of financial reporting rests not in a particular disclosure or sales practice or single accounting technique.

* * *

Too many CFO's are being judged today not by how effectively they manage operations, but by how they manage the Street. Too many analysts are being judged not by how well they analyze a particular company, but by how well they assist in selling the latest deal. And too many auditors are being judged not just by how well they manage an audit, but by how well they cross-market their firm's non-audit services. Amidst this pressure * * *, safeguarding the independence of the accounting profession has never been more critical.

Why Independence Matters

Independence is at the core of the profession, the very essence that gives an auditor's work its value. It is the space and the freedom to think, to speak, and to act on the truth. And truth is the lifeblood of investor confidence.

Today, the accounting profession stands at a pivotal moment in its history. During the last several months, you've no doubt noticed stories detailing broad reorganizations of the largest and most prestigious accounting firms. These proposals, designed to monetize some or all of the firms' consulting businesses, have the potential to advance the public interest by returning the core focus to accounting and auditing. But these constructive divestitures of consulting businesses must be accomplished without creating conflicts of interest through long-term financial relationships.

More than five decades ago, one of the profession's own said, "The accounting profession must be like Caesar's wife. To be suspected is almost as bad as to be convicted." There has always been this higher standard for the auditor. It is not enough that the accountant on an engagement act independently. For investors to have confidence in the quality of the audit, the public must perceive the accountant as independent.

Independence, at its most basic level, is exercised and honored by those professionals who must abide by it, and assumed by those who must rely on it. It is a covenant between auditor and investor, and no one else; a covenant that says the auditor works in the interests of shareholders, not on behalf of management; a covenant that says the auditor must steer clear of having financial interests in the companies he or she audits; and a covenant that says the auditor's work stands separate and apart from their clients' business. These are the basic principles that have established the foundation of independence for more than six decades.

Transformation of a Profession

Yet, a tension within the profession between its commercial aspirations and its commitment to the public interest has existed almost from its inception. Over the past forty years, the profession has struggled with how to properly and effectively enshrine the values of independence while maintaining its competitive edge. And, as the forces of consolidation, globalization and product line expansion continued to transform the biggest accounting firms, a debate over the role of the auditor – and the inherent pressures of practicing within a firm offering clients a range of other professional services – became more acute.

In fact, today, auditing no longer dominates the practices of the largest firms. It accounts for just 30 percent of total revenues – down from 70 percent in 1977. Consulting and other management advisory services now represent over half – up from 12 percent in 1977. Since 1993, auditing revenues have been growing by 9 percent per year on average – while consulting and similar services have been growing at a rate of 27 percent each year.

It's no wonder that the Big 5 now position themselves globally as "multidisciplinary professional service organizations" rather than accounting firms. Among the expanded menu of services the major firms provide today are corporate finance, risk management, actuarial work, merger and acquisition analysis, network and database architecture, and asset management in addition to traditional accounting, auditing and tax work.

Serving Two Masters

As the firms expand their product lines, consulting and other services may shorten the distance between the auditor and management. Independence – if not in fact, then certainly in appearance – becomes a more elusive proposition. When an audit firm performs valuations of numbers that appear in its client's financials, the mandate for independence is threatened. When an audit firm performs the internal audit function its client would otherwise do, the ethic of independence is tarnished. When an audit firm also keeps its clients books, the principle of independence is undermined. And when some firms take on tax and other assignments where the size of the fee is based on the answer given, one has to wonder how such a practice is consistent with a culture that has long prided itself on objectivity.

Not surprisingly, product line expansion has been an outgrowth of market forces. And the audit is sometimes priced lower to attract clients willing to pay for higher margin consulting services. But, the audit foothold as a distribution channel is at the very root of the inherent tension that these interdependent relationships foster. The audit engagement partner, upon whose shoulders much of the credibility of the profession rests, makes decisions each day that affect the underlying quality of the audit. These often unrecognized guardians of our capital markets exercise the judgment that validates the integrity of the financial information.

More than a hundred years ago, it was said, "A public accountant acknowledges no master but the public." But, when auditors engage in extensive services for an audit client truly unrelated to the audit, they must now also serve another master – management. In this dual role, the auditor, who guards the integrity of the numbers, now both oversees and answers to management.

Assuming the role of "relationship" manager, the auditor helps develop and coordinate extensive cross-selling and marketing strategies with, for example, his firm's information technology consulting group. And while it may never be quite so explicit, some auditors know, and others suspect, that their compensation is influenced by how well they "manage" that relationship in its entirety. As the firms' business objectives drive them into broader alliances, it's becoming more difficult to ascertain where one relationship ends and another begins. Some may argue that this is not an enlightened or realistic view of the marketplace. Increasingly complex audits require that firms branch out and develop greater and more diverse expertise. The profession, some say, must rely on its consulting business to attract and retain the best and brightest talent; that no direct link between consulting services and audit failures has ever been proven; and, more fundamentally, that a firm's motivation to protect its reputational capital serves as a sufficient inducement to act in the public interest.

Now, I recognize that new financial instruments, new technologies and even new markets demand more specialized know-how to effectively audit many of today's companies. If a firm is auditing a major computer company or a global financial services firm, it needs to have the necessary technological or financial skills. And, as technology becomes increasingly important to business and to the future of the profession, firms need to be able to develop and maintain these essential skills. When this broader skill set is being used to further the audit, that's good business and good for investors. But if those skills are used purely to build databases, structure employment payment plans, or devise financial strategies, I'm concerned that the audit function is simply being used as a springboard to more lucrative consulting services – instead of augmenting the firm's core focus.

Some argue that offering consulting services to audit clients facilitates the recruitment of talented professionals. But if these same services can be offered to other clients, isn't this more an argument for the synergies of a business model based on cross-selling services? In any event, a more competitive recruiting environment is not sufficient justification to awaken the specter of compromise or to jeopardize the integrity of audits.

One can't help but think that a renewed focus on auditing will generate greater recruitment and retention success. With the training and knowledge of world class business practices, and competitive financial rewards, I have no doubt that auditing will continue to be an exceptional "proving ground" for America's young professionals. What's more, the need to reinvest in the audit is more important than ever in order to meet the demands of greater information and more complex businesses.

And finally, some say that appearance simply doesn't matter; that auditors should be free to perform almost any service unless it can be proven that a business or financial relationship directly undermines the audit. But that view misses one of the most important aspects of an auditor's responsibilities. It is not the bright line of right and wrong that the lack of auditor independence often implicates as much as it is that grey area where the answers aren't so clear; where the temptation to "see it the way your client does" is subtle, yet real.

Independence is, in many respects, a condition of the mind of the auditor, its reflection the trust and confidence of the public. To suggest that we should wait to experience erosion before we act to preserve this confidence is to ignore the wisdom of Benjamin Franklin, "Glass, china, and reputation are easily cracked, and never mended well."

Working Towards a Solution

This nation's public accounting firms have been granted a unique and privileged franchise – a franchise that tells investors, "I stand with you." Questioning the dedication to that franchise is not the point. Preserving it is.

New and diverse revenue streams have created a mix of business relationships so unprecedented in breadth and scope, it's long past time to address meaningfully the effect all of this is having on a culture that has long prided itself on objectivity.

The Chairman of one major firm recently said that the pending sale of his firm's consulting practice is "the right thing to do." And the firm's clients have responded positively to its reaffirmation of the audit. This recognition of the importance of the audit and independence concerns – and taking action to alleviate these concerns – represents business statesmanship. This is a significant benchmark towards a workable solution.

Several others are considering similar responses to this growing issue and the Commission will endeavor to be constructive in expediting such actions. Others have raised "firewalls" as a way to minimize potential conflicts despite a sharing of profits and other links. I'm not so sure this provides sufficient protection.

In the coming months, the Commission will consider how to address the long-term ramifications of today's restructurings on both auditor independence and investor confidence. In my view, any regulatory action must address a few fundamental public policy questions: Should there be more appropriate limits on the types of services that an audit firm can render to a public company client? How should audit firms be structured to assure independence? What are the consequences, if any, of public ownership? Should firms be permitted to affiliate with entities who provide services to the firms' audit clients that the firms themselves would not be allowed to provide?

There are at least three possible ways to address these potential conflicts. Many in the profession once sought to establish broad "principles" of independence. Alternatively, greater public disclosure of the types and amounts of services offered could be required. Or, certain services considered inconsistent with an independent public audit could be prohibited. Each of these alternatives, as one might expect, has both advantages and drawbacks.

While principles may sound "high-minded," the lack of precision may not address the level of uncertainty as to which services are permissible and which ones are not. A public disclosure-based model, already used in the UK, could be worthwhile for certain types of perceived conflicts if such disclosure doesn't devolve into meaningless boilerplate.

Perhaps a more reliable way to safeguard independence would be to clearly define those consulting services that compromise the integrity of the audit without adding meaningful benefits to that audit. Like any rules, however, such an approach entails a degree of definitional precision.

While a "perfect" solution may not exist, that's no reason to sit back and do nothing. A careful balance of "bright line" rules establishing clear limits, coupled with greater disclosure, seems both warranted and prudent. But, even before the SEC considers ways to safeguard independence, I appeal to corporate America's audit committees to pay close attention to the types of services their auditors are performing and to question whether it would be more in their investors' interests to have some of those services performed by someone else.

The Golden Rule of Auditing

In recent months, one aspect of auditor independence called into question involves the golden rule of auditing: auditors cannot invest in their clients. Many of you, I'm sure, are aware of the widespread violations of the financial interest rules by one of the largest and most respected firms.

There is no doubt that certain violations were the result of a large merger, rapid expansion, and a system of less than modern rules of the profession and the SEC. The most significant public policy issue was never the egregiousness of any particular violation, but rather, the inadequacy of internal controls. In the aftermath of that difficult period, I've been encouraged by the response. That firm is working constructively with the SEC and undertaking significant modernizing efforts by investing in better systems and training.

To eliminate the lingering doubt on the profession from this episode, and in response to evidence of similar problems at other firms, the Commission's staff requested that the Public Oversight Board, an entity charged with oversight of the profession, undertake a special review of larger member firms' current compliance with SEC and profession independence rules. I'm pleased that these firms appear to be moving ahead with substantial commitments of money and resources towards implementing more effective systems.

* * *

I'm sensitive to the demographic and business changes that have occurred over the last two decades, as well as their implications for overly strict rules on financial investments. I couldn't agree more with those who maintain that certain rules extending to retirement plans and relatives don't make sense today. We also need to reform those rules that unfairly impose burdens on dual-career families without a commensurate benefit to the investing public. The Independence Standards Board * * * recently has taken a significant and positive step towards reform. We at the SEC are committed to doing our part. But amidst this change, firms must remain committed to ensuring that their internal controls, like those of the clients they audit, identify and prevent the very failings they were designed to guard against.

Once again, I appeal to audit committee members to sit down with their auditors and inquire about past compliance and current safeguards to prevent such conflicts in the future.

A Case for Stronger, Independent Oversight of the Profession

More than three decades ago, Leonard Spacek, a visionary accounting industry leader, stated that, "You and I cannot survive as a group, obtaining the confidence of the public in our work, unless as a profession we have a workable plan of self-regulation."

Fourteen years after Leonard Spacek's comment, the profession implemented what it viewed as one of the most ambitious self-regulatory programs ever adopted. While this was a significant step forward, the Commission, and many in Congress, still had their doubts. "The jury is out," then SEC Chairman Harold Williams stated in 1978 upon the creation of the [Public Oversight Board], "on whether [this] program of self-regulation will be successful."

In the midst of ever more complicated audit engagements and interwoven business relationships, it's become abundantly clear that a more modern and effective approach to self-regulation in the accounting profession today is an absolute necessity. Indeed, more effective oversight must be brought to bear on the profession's trade group, the AICPA, which seems unable to discipline its own members for violations of its own standards of professional conduct.

In my time at the Commission, I have come to appreciate the important role played by an independent oversight program. But, I am also aware of its limitations. In the last few months, however, a real opportunity emerged to give the POB the independence and the freedom to fully discharge its public responsibilities, unfettered by special interests.

The POB, under the leadership of Charles Bowsher, former Comptroller General of the United States, and with the support of its other distinguished members, has put forth a plan to modernize the profession's oversight and reinforce its commitment to the public interest. But this is only possible if the industry's leaders recognize and accept the importance of a truly independent oversight body.

By nature, I'm an optimist. And in helping to champion this plan for reform, I am encouraged. But it could be undermined by those who either fail to grasp the benefits of public confidence that arise from meaningful oversight, or who view reform with a sense of foreboding.

It is hard for me to fathom continuing industry resistance to the POB's plan. Can you really have meaningful oversight without giving the POB input into the profession's regulatory boards and its rulemaking and guidance mechanisms? Can you really deny the public's right to greater access through annual reports, special reports, and minutes of meetings? Can you really deny the POB the right to have "no strings" funding and the authority to conduct appropriate special reviews of firms' practices?

* * *

Action Plan

Our system of financial reporting remains second to none in creating transparency, in limiting cost of capital, and in enhancing accountability. We must guard that preeminence with an ever present vigilance. Today, I am calling on key participants in the financial reporting process – companies, their audit committees, and the accounting profession – to join with the Commission in addressing issues that so clearly threaten to erode a fundamental underpinning of confidence in America's capital markets.

A Challenge for the Accounting Profession and Its Regulators

Learn From the Past. I challenge all the leaders of the major accounting firms to work with the Commission to develop a plan for constructively assessing the firms' past compliance with financial investment rules. Based on recent discussions, I am hopeful that we can soon reach agreement with several of the major firms. In addition, we ask that the profession continue to modernize its system of controls both domestically and on a worldwide basis, and for the POB to oversee and report on this progress. For our part, we pledge to use this information to help improve compliance systems in the future and not to punish minor, past mistakes.

Updating the Independence Framework. In addition, as the Commission's Chief Accountant stated in January, we commit to work with the profession and the Independence Standards Board to undertake in short order a long overdue modernization of certain financial investment rules. To do that, I commit that modernization will be as important a priority as the other initiatives we are discussing * * *, and I'm asking the staff to submit a rulemaking proposal to the Commission on this issue by summer.

Creating Stronger, More Effective Oversight. I also strongly endorse the notion of enhanced POB oversight of the accounting profession, and urge the profession to endorse it as well. Public confidence is not to be taken lightly. And effective, independent oversight is a signal avenue to foster and preserve that confidence. A revised charter setting forth what the present POB thinks it needs to get the job done is before the profession. The time for action is now.

And, since independence is so important to the integrity of this profession, I also believe the time has come to obtain majority public representation on the ISB.

Rebuilding the Accounting Profession's Business Model Around Independence. Lastly, I am asking the SEC staff to prepare a rulemaking initiative on how best to deal with the conflicts created by the profession's ever-expanding menu of services offered to public company audit clients. The rulemaking initiative should also look at firm affiliations and strategic alliances. I anticipate that any resulting rule proposal will be supplemented by public hearings to garner the broadest possible input.

Conclusion

It wasn't too long ago when the refrain, "Where were the accountants?" echoed loudly through the halls of corporations, the floors of the markets and the living rooms of many American families. We sometimes take for granted the freedom and power of independent thought and action. And only after it's been compromised, do we fully realize how fundamental it is to the pursuit of economic opportunity.

Independence is a basic American ideal. It is a basic value and a basic requirement for fair and efficient markets to exist. I have talked about conflicts of interest. I have talked about compliance controls. I have talked about oversight powers. I have talked about cross-selling and the audit function. We can use labels, rationales, or justifications to argue why an auditor's independence is so important.

But in the final analysis, it's the pensioner who reads her monthly statement walking back from the mail box; it's the young college student who buys his first stock; it's the young couple who start a college fund for their new daughter; it's the manager of a firefighter or teacher retirement fund; it is every person who is the fabric of our markets who doesn't have to think twice about the quality of the numbers. The profession's independence gives American investors their independence by instilling a systemic confidence throughout our marketplace.

Confidence is not a measurable commodity that can be either mandated or purchased. Rather, it is a quality, an amalgam of beliefs, convictions, sensibilities that ultimately are the result of experience. Once lost, this fragile but strong characteristic is almost impossible to rehabilitate.

America's accountants have been both the beneficiaries and the source of investors' acceptance of the sanctity of reported numbers. This profession, dating back to the 15th century, has a tradition of fidelity to the public interest[.] We will safeguard this heritage by determining that the independent audit is not a means to anything else, but rather, a critically important end in itself. We will build on our past by being certain that independent oversight is so fundamentally a part of the industry's culture that it removes any uncertainty or doubt. We will give resonance to our markets when a critical self awareness of the past provides guidance for the future. This is our collective mandate, and I ask the leaders of the accounting profession to join in ensuring the profession's future is worthy of its past.

NOTES

1. We have already observed that management, either directly or indirectly, usually selects the auditing firm. Although the SEC's regulations on auditor changes have curtailed a registrant's ability to "opinion shop," management can still apply pressure on auditors to approve, or at least acquiesce in, questionable accounting treatments, particularly when GAAP offers some discretion in selecting an accounting principle. At least theoretically, management can threaten to hire another firm to perform the non-audit services unless the auditor accepts certain accounting treatments. *See generally* Daniel L. Goelzer, *The SEC and Opinion Shopping: A Case Study in the Changing Regulation of the Accounting Profession*, 52 Brook. L. Rev. 1057 (1987) (recognizing that competition to provide both audit and nonaudit services has affected longstanding relationships between auditors and clients); *see also* Lorie Soares, Note, *The Big Eight, Management Consulting and Independence: Myth or Reality?*, 61 S. CAL. L. REV. 1511 (1988).

2. SEC rules and professional standards regarding independence recently forced many of the 140,000 employees of Price Waterhouse and Coopers & Lybrand to sell investments in the audit clients of the other firm prior to the merger which created PricewaterhouseCoopers. *See* In re Goodbread, Accounting and Auditing Enforcement Release No. 861, 7 Fed. Sec. L. Rep. (CCH) ¶ 74,376 (1996) (partner censured for failing to sell 400 shares in audit client immediately following 1989 merger between Touche Ross and Deloitte, Haskins & Sells, which created Deloitte & Touche); *but see* Robbins v. Koger Properties, Inc., 116 F.3d 1441 (11th Cir. 1997) (reversing a jury verdict against Deloitte for more than $81 million in a securities fraud case arising from the same audit and rendering judgment in Deloitte's favor because plaintiffs did not offer sufficient proof of loss causation). These partners and audit employees faced limited options for reinvesting the proceeds from these sales because the merged firm will audit about a quarter of all publicly traded companies and more than half the mutual funds in the United States. Anne Tergesen, *In an Accounting Merger, Stock Must Go, So Workers Face Tax Bills*, N.Y. Times, June 28, 1998, sec. 3, at 4.

In fact, however, Coopers & Lybrand's retirement plan did not timely sell the securities of thirty-two PricewaterhouseCoopers ("PWC") publicly traded audit clients that Price Waterhouse had audited before the merger. In almost fifty other situations that occurred between 1996 and 1998: (i) certain professionals at Coopers & Lybrand owned securities of publicly held audit clients for which they performed professional services; (ii) partners or managers owned securities of public companies for which they provided no professional services, but which the firm audited; or (iii) Coopers & Lybrand's retirement plan held securities of publicly traded audit clients. As a result, and without admitting or denying the misconduct, PWC recently agreed to various remedial sanctions to settle administrative charges that the firm violated the SEC's auditor independence rules. The firm accepted a censure and agreed to establish a $2.5 million fund which will further awareness and education throughout the profession relating to the independence requirement for public accounting firms; to improve its internal procedures for monitoring adherence to auditor independence rules; and to conduct an internal investigation. In re PricewaterhouseCoopers LLP, Accounting and Auditing Enforcement Release No. 1098, 7 Fed. Sec. L. Rep. (CCH) ¶ 74,605 (1999). The internal investigation subsequently revealed that 1885 professionals committed a total of 8064 infractions over a two-year period involving 2159 clients. In particular, close to half of PWC's almost 2,700 partners self-reported at least one independence violation, that each reporting partner disclosed an average of five violations, and that more than 150 partners reported more than ten violations. In addition, random tests found that more than three-quarters of PWC partners failed to self-report at least one independence violation. Public Oversight Board, Annual Report 1999, at 5 (2000); Phyllis Diamond, *Consultant Report on PWC Finds Widespread Independence Violations*, 32 Sec. Reg. & L. Rep. (BNA) 31, 32 (2000).

3.   Other situations when auditors have compromised independence include preparing the financial statements under audit, simultaneously representing the client as an attorney, participating in an audit after accepting an employment offer from the client, and accepting business or personal loans from a client. *See, e.g.*, In re Broadbent, Accounting and Auditing Enforcement Release No. 921, [1995-1998 Accounting and Auditing Enforcement Releases Transfer Binder] Fed. Sec. L. Rep. (CCH) ¶ 74,436 (1997) (auditor prepared the financial statements he was auditing and performed bookkeeping services for client); In re Hein + Associates LLP, Accounting & Auditing Enforcement Release No. 798, [1991-1995 Accounting and Auditing Enforcement Releases Transfer Binder] Fed. Sec. L. Rep. (CCH) ¶ 74,313 (1996) (auditor continued to participate in audit after accepting employment with client); In re Greenspan, Accounting and Auditing Release No. 312, [1987-1991 Accounting and Auditing Enforcement Releases Transfer Binder] Fed. Sec. L. Rep. (CCH) ¶ 73,781 (1991) (auditor represented client and also served as "of counsel" to law firm that represented client on corporate and securities matters while performing audit services); SEC v. Ernst & Young, Accounting and Auditing Enforcement Release No. 301, [1987-1991 Accounting and Auditing Enforcement Releases Transfer Binder] Fed. Sec. L. Rep. (CCH) ¶ 73,770 (1991) (at least twenty-seven partners in accounting firm had obtained more than $5 million in personal loans and over fifty partners belonged to real estate partnerships that had borrowed at least $15.8 million from audit client); see also *Ernst & Young Settles SEC Case Alleging Lack Of Auditor Independence*, 27 Sec. Reg. & L. Rep. (BNA) 483 (1995). In reaction to this last situation, the AICPA amended its Code of Professional Conduct, effective January 1, 1992, to restrict auditors from accepting loans from financial institution clients. Exceptions apply to automobile loans and leases, credit card and cash advances which do not each exceed $5,000 in the aggregate, and certain loans which cash deposits secure. *AICPA Bars Accountants From Accepting Virtually All Loans From Audit Clients*, 23 Sec. Reg. & L. Rep. (BNA) 1457 (1991).

4. Outside the United States, especially in Europe, major mergers and alliances have already occurred between accounting and law firms as they seek to form global multidisciplinary practices ("MDPs"). In particular, accounting firms increasingly hire lawyers to provide various services for clients in an effort to become more "full service." Clients increasingly desire comprehensive solutions to their problems and opportunities and prefer so-called "one-stop shopping."   In a recent letter to the American Bar Association, which has been studying whether to amend the Model Rules of Professional Conduct to allow lawyers to share legal fees with non-lawyers, the SEC did not take any position against MDPs per se. The SEC, however, did state that its independence rules prohibit an auditor from certifying an enterprise's financial statements if the auditor also has entered into an attorney-client relationship with the enterprise. For years, the SEC has held the position "that 'the attorney-client relationship is inconsistent with the independence of accountants in reporting to investors.'" Paul Rootare, *First Ever Ethics Panel Addresses Hot Topics: Accounting Recklessness Rules; Pay-to-Play*, 32 Sec. Reg. & L. Rep. (BNA) 368, 369 (2000).   *See also* Eileen J. Williams, *Globalization, Consolidation Spurring Multidisciplinary Trends, Changing Face of Legal, Accounting Firms, Practitioners Say*, Corp. Counsel Weekly, Mar. 31, 1999, at 8; Elizabeth MacDonald, *Accounting Firms Hire Lawyers And Other Attorneys Cry Foul*, Wall St. J., Aug. 22, 1997, at B8; *see also* John Gibeaut, *Squeeze Play*, ABA J., Feb. 1998, at 42-47 (discussing accountants' movement into the legal market); Gianluca Morello, *Note, Big Six Accounting Firms Shop Worldwide for Law Firms: Why Multi-Discipline Practices Should Be Permitted in the United States*, 21 Fordham Int'l L.J. 190, 198-203 (1997) (same). If a firm lawfully renders what attorneys might consider legal services to an audit client, do those professional services impair the auditor's independence?

5. One commentator recently set forth two alternatives for examining the auditor independence standards. Under the first view, the independence standards serve as necessary constraints that the SEC, ISB or AICPA impose. As a result, an auditor might understandably try to maneuver around or barely satisfy such externally imposed constraints. Under the second view, independence, along with expertise in measurement and competence in application of standardized measurement rules, function as three core values that sustain auditors' individual and collective reputations. This second view would suggest that auditors should try to develop, maintain and exploit this core value. William R. Kinney, Jr., *Auditor Independence: A Burdensome Constraint or Core Value*, 13 Acct. Horizons 69 (1999). Auditors, regulators, scholars, as well as lawyers, might keep these alternative views in mind as the ongoing debate on independence continues.

6. For a recent article examining SEC disciplinary decisions and judicial rulings adverse to accountants who have violated independence standards during the period from 1980 to September 1998, see Paul R. Brown, Jeanne A. Calderon & Baruch Lev, *Administrative and Judicial Approaches to Auditor Indpendence*, 30 SETON HALL L. REV. 443 (2000).

Page 158. At the end of the carryover paragraph, insert the following new material:

In 1997, and in response to the previously described developments within the industry, the SEC and the AICPA announced the creation of a separate panel within the AICPA, the Independence Standards Board ("ISB"), to establish independence standards for auditors of registrants in an attempt to protect and promote investors' confidence in the U.S. securities markets. A later section of this update describes the ISB and its charge in greater detail. See *infra* at 31-32.

In another development, the SEC instituted public administrative proceedings in 1997 to determine if KPMG Peat Marwick ("KPMG") engaged in improper professional conduct and violated the federal securities laws during its audit of the 1995 financial statements for Porta Systems Corp. ("Porta"), a financially troubled client. The case illustrates the complex business relationships often found in the accounting industry today. About January 1995, KPMG organized and lent large sums to KPMG Baymark ("Baymark"), a firm that Edward R. Olson and three others owned, and two operating subsidiaries. According to the SEC, KPMG planned to use Baymark as a business structure to engage in the "corporate turnaround" business. A contract between KPMG and Baymark required the latter to pay KPMG five percent of its consolidated fee income. Later in 1995, and as part of a turnaround engagement, which entitled Baymark's operating subsidiary to a $250,000 management fee and a contingent success fee based upon Porta's quarterly earnings, disposed inventory and restructured debt, Baymark installed Olson as Porta's President and Chief Operating Officer. According to the SEC's complaint, the Office of the Chief Accountant cautioned KPMG about its apparent lack of independence during late 1995 and early 1996. The SEC alleged that KPMG lacked independence both in fact and in appearance during the 1995 audit because the firm: (1) had loaned $100,000 to Olson, who was serving as the audit client's President and Chief Operating Officer; (2) had capitalized Baymark, not only a business in which Olson owned a twenty-five percent interest, but also an "affiliate" of the audit client under the federal securities laws; (3) held a contingent right to receive revenues based on Porta's success. Based upon the contractual ties between KPMG and Baymark, the SEC's Division of Enforcement and Office of the Chief Accountant alleged that the SEC should consider KPMG and Baymark as a single entity for independence purposes. In re KPMG Peat Marwick LLP, Accounting and Auditing Enforcement Release No. 994, [1995-1998 Accounting and Auditing Enforcement Releases Transfer Binder] Fed. Sec. L. Rep. (CCH) ¶ 74,509 (1997). After an administrative hearing, an administrative law judge concluded that although the loan to Olson violated the independence rules and that KPMG's lack of independence caused Porta Systems to violate the annual reporting requirements in the federal securities laws, the record did not establish that KPMG recklessly engaged in improper professional conduct. In addition, the ALJ denied the Division of Enforcement's request for a cease and desist order. In re KPMG Peat Marwick L.L.P., 71 S.E.C. Docket 1220 (2000).

b. THE AUDIT PROCESS

Page 159. At the end of the first full paragraph, insert the following discussion:

Following several high profile financial frauds that raised questions about the audit process because auditors failed to detect seriously misstated financial statements and at SEC Chairman Arthur Levitt's urging, the Public Oversight Board established a special panel on audit effectiveness in October 1998. In June 2000, the special panel issued a draft report that describes both the auditing profession and the quality of its audits as "fundamentally sound." In an effort to improve the reliability and credibility of financial statements and to help maintain investor confidence, however, the report offers several significant recommendations. Perhaps most significantly, the panel recommends that auditors perform some "forensic-type" procedures in every audit to enhance the prospects of detecting material fraud in the financial statements. In addition, the panel encourages the Auditing Standards Board to issue more specific and definitive auditing and quality control standards; urges audit committees to pre-approve non-audit services that exceed a threshold amount; advocates that audit firms put more emphasis on the performance of high quality audits in communications from top management, performance evaluations, training, and compensation and promotion decisions; and urges the International Federation of Accountants to establish an international self-regulatory system for the auditing profession. Public Oversight Board, Panel on Audit Effectiveness Report and Recommendations (Exposure Draft–May 31, 2000) (available at <http://www.pobauditpanel.org>) .

2. THE ESTABLISHMENT OF GENERALLY ACCEPTED AUDITING STANDARDS

a. SECURITIES AND EXCHANGE COMMISSION

Page 164. Insert the following discussion before the carryover paragraph at the bottom of the page:

Most recently, and as already mentioned, the SEC convinced the AICPA to establish the ISB in 1997. Early in the following year, and consistent with the SEC's continuing policy of looking to the private sector for leadership in establishing and improving accounting principles and auditing standards, the SEC issued a financial reporting release which formally announced the agency's plans to look to the ISB, as the standard-setting body that the accounting profession has designated, to establish and maintain a body of independence standards applicable to the auditors of all SEC registrants for at least a five year period. The release states that in reviewing questions related to whether an auditor qualifies as independent in fact or in appearance from an audit client, the SEC will consider principles, standards, interpretations and practices that the ISB has set or established as having "substantial authoritative support." The Commission, however, expressly retains its statutory authority regarding auditor independence, including its authority to bring enforcement actions and to reject, modify or supplement ISB independence standards and interpretations in the same way that the SEC can modify or supplement FASB pronouncements. Within five years after the ISB's establishment, the SEC will evaluate the ISB's operations and determine whether the new framework serves the public interest and protects investors. Financial Reporting Release No. 50, The

Establishment and Improvement of Standards Related to Auditor Independence, 63
Fed. Reg. 9135 (1998), codified in the Codification of Financial Reporting Policies, §
601.04, reprinted in 7 Fed. Sec. L. Rep. (CCH) ¶ 73,254 (Mar. 25, 1998).

**Page 165. Replace the remainder of the paragraph that begins with the
sentence on the twentieth line with the following:**

In response to this legislation, the SEC adopted an amendment to Regulation S-X to
define the term "[a]udit (or examination)" so that the Commission may modify or
supplement generally accepted auditing standards. The related financial reporting
release expressed the SEC's desire to alert auditors and issuers to the possibility
that, in certain circumstances, the Commission may mandate additional audit
procedures, beyond those that GAAS require. In addition, the SEC specifically
rejected objections to the amendment on the ground that the statute limits the
Commission's ability to set auditing standards to the three areas enumerated in the
legislation. Financial Reporting Release No. 49, Implementation of Section 10A of
the Securities Exchange Act of 1934, 62 Fed. Reg. 12743 (1997), codified at 17 C.F.R.
§ 210.1-02(d) (adopted Mar. 18, 1997); *see also* Shelene Clark, *Securities Litigation
Reform Act's Impact Questionable; Struggle With Law's Interpretation Seen in
Coming Years*, Corp. Counsel Weekly, Apr. 10, 1996, at 6.

b. THE ACCOUNTING PROFESSION

**Page 166. Replace the third sentence in the second paragraph under this
heading with the following:**

As of April 30, 2000, AudSEC and its successor, the ASB, had published ninety
Statements on Auditing Standards ("SASs").

**Page 166. Insert the following discussion about the Independence
Standards Board at the bottom of the page:**

In 1997, and with the SEC's approval and support, the AICPA created the ISB
to establish independence standards for auditors of public companies, an effort
labeled as a "new public-private sector partnership." The part-time and eight-person
board, which typically meets quarterly, currently includes four public or
"independent" members, described as "prominent individuals of high integrity and
reputation, who understand the importance of investor protection, the U.S. capital
markets, and the accounting profession," and four practicing CPAs. The board must
elect its chairman, currently former Delaware Chancery Court Chancellor William
Allen, from the public members. In recent remarks, SEC Chairman Arthur Levitt
has called for a majority of public or "independent" members on the ISB. Steve
Burkholder, *Levitt Urges Majority of Public-Oriented Members on ISB*, 32 Sec. Reg.
& L. Rep. (BNA) 651 (2000).

Under the ISB's due process procedures, the board conducts standard-setting meetings in public and will expose proposed standards for public comment. Representatives from the SEC attend ISB meetings and can speak at those meetings. Similar to its relationship with FASB, the SEC expects to oversee the ISB, review draft standards, and discuss standard setting, interpretive and procedure issues with the ISB members and staff. The AICPA agreed to provide funding for the board and its full-time executive director and staff.

Using the Emerging Issues Task Force ("EITF") as a model, the ISB has established a nine-member panel, the Independence Issues Committee ("IIC"), to identify emerging issues for ISB's consideration, interpret rules and publish consensus positions. Unlike the EITF, however, IIC can perform other duties, such as conduct research, that the ISB may assign. The ISB's Executive Director serves as the IIC's non-voting chairman. ISB's rules require seven of the nine members, all CPAs, to approve any consensus positions. To assure participation by the ISB's public members, the ISB must approve any position of the ISB staff or consensus position before that position or consensus becomes generally authoritative. *ISB Names Emerging Issues Panel*, 29 Sec. Reg. & L. Rep. (BNA) 1538 (1997); *SEC Reports to Dingell on Operation Of New Panel on Auditor Independence*, 29 Sec. Reg. & L. Rep. (BNA) 1310 (1997); *SEC, AICPA Announce New Panel To Set Auditor Independence Standards*, 29 Sec. Reg. & L. Rep. (BNA) 720 (1997).

As of April 30, 2000, ISB had formally adopted the SEC staff's rulings on auditor independence and approved two standards and two interpretations. The first standard requires "independent accountants" under the federal securities laws to confirm, in writing, their independence from the enterprises that they audit and to discuss that conclusion with each client's audit committee, or board of directors if no audit committee exists. The ISB's current agenda includes efforts to develop a conceptual framework and rule-making projects on evolving forms of firm structure and organization in the professional services community to respond to the recent trend where companies, such as American Express, add auditing entities to their financial services operations; appraisal and valuation services; what "legal" services, if any, an auditor can perform for an audit client; family relationships that arise when an auditor's relative serves as an executive or other manager for an audit client; and the "revolving door" problem, namely situations in which a partner or staff member of an accounting firm leaves the firm to become an employee of the audit client.

c. INTERNATIONAL AUDITING STANDARDS

Page 167. Replace the first paragraph of this section with the following:

Even if some body or organization promulgates a core set of international accounting principles that gain worldwide acceptance, those principles will not achieve their purpose unless adequate auditing and enforcement ensure their application. Pursuant to its mission to develop and enhance an accounting profession "able to provide services of consistently high quality in the public interest," the International Federation of Accountants ("IFAC"), a group of 128 national professional accountancy bodies, including the AICPA, from ninety-one countries, representing two million accountants, has formed the International Auditing Practices Committee ("IAPC") to develop and issue standards and statements on auditing and related services. IAPC issues International Standards on Auditing ("ISAs") and International Auditing Practice Statements ("IASPs") and seeks to promote their voluntary acceptance. ISAs describe basic principles and essential procedures and offer guidance through explanatory and other material. In contrast, IASPs provide practical assistance to auditors in implementing ISAs or promoting good practice. IASPs enjoy less authority than ISAs. Neither ISAs nor IASPs, however, establish standards which auditors must follow under the AICPA's Code of Professional Conduct. Before an ISA or related IASP will apply to audits in the United States, the ASB must specifically adopt the ISA. In addition, IFAC has developed a Code of Ethics for Professional Accountants to serve as an ethical model for the profession. American Institute of Certified Public Accountants, 2 Professional Standards, at AU §§ 8100, 11,100 (June 1998); Steve Burkholder, *International Accountants Group Issue Draft Auditing Guidance on Y2K*, 30 Sec. Reg. & L. Rep. (BNA) 431 (1998).

5. THE EXPECTATION GAP

Page 171. At the end of the carryover paragraph at the top of the page, insert the following:

One recent example may illustrate how a quantitatively immaterial item might nevertheless qualify as material. An October 1998 *Wall Street Journal* article describes BankAmerica Corp.'s failure to disclose information about its $372 million write-down of a loan to D.E. Shaw & Co., a New York investment firm. Even though bank officials knew about possible losses on the loan as early as August, the bank did not disclose the extent of the losses before shareholders voted in late September to approve a $43 billion merger with NationsBank, which created the nation's second-largest bank. The article quotes the merged bank's chief financial officer as saying that "'[$372 million is] a big number but it's not material to a company' that is as big as Bank America." When the merged bank announced the write-down in mid-October, the stock price dropped eleven percent in a single day. Rick Brooks & Mitchell Pacelle, *BankAmerica Knew in August of Trading Woes*, Wall St. J., Oct. 16, 1998, at A3.

In Staff Accounting Bulletin No. 99, the SEC's staff explicitly rejected the automatic classification of financial statement misstatements or omissions that fall under a five percent threshold as immaterial, absent particularly egregious circumstances, such as misappropriation by senior management. The staff emphasized that registrants and their auditors must consider qualitative factors in materiality determinations. For example, a quantitatively small misstatement or omission could nevertheless qualify as material when it:

- arises from an item capable of precise measurement;

- masks a change in earnings or other trends;

- hides a failure to meet analysts' consensus expectations for the enterprise,

- changes a loss into income or vice versa;

- concerns a segment or other portion of the registrant's business that has been identified as playing a significant role in the registrant's operations or profitability;

- determines the registrant's compliance with regulatory requirements;

- affects the registrant's compliance with loan covenants or other contractual requirements;

- increases management's compensation – for example, by satisfying requirement for the award of bonuses or other forms of incentive compensation; or

- involves concealment of an unlawful transaction.

In assessing multiple misstatements, the bulletin reminds registrants and auditors that they must consider all misstatements or omissions both separately and in the aggregate to determine whether, in relation to the individual line item amounts, subtotals or totals in the financial statements, the misstatements or omissions materially misstate the financial statements taken as a whole. Finally, the SAB reminds registrants that immaterial, but intentional misstatements can violate the federal securities laws. Materiality, Staff Accounting Bulletin No. 99, 64 Fed. Reg. 45,150 (1999), reprinted in 7 Fed. Sec. L. Rep. (CCH) ¶ 75,501, at 64,219-3 (Dec. 8, 1999); *see also* Kenneth C. Fang & Brad Jacobs, *Clarifying and Protecting Materiality Standards in Financial Statements: A Review of SEC Staff Accounting Bulletin 99*, 55 BUS. LAW. 1039 (2000) (tracing the development of materiality standards, examining the purpose and reasoning behind SAB No. 99's release, and concluding that the bulletin creates an ambiguous standard that opens the door to liability for innocent mistakes in judgment).

b. THE AUDITOR'S RESPONSIBILITY TO DETECT AND REPORT ERRORS, FRAUD AND ILLEGAL ACTS

Page 173-174. Replace everything starting with the last sentence and related citations in the first paragraph on page 173 and up to the "Audit Reports" heading on page 174 with the following:

The SEC has issued final regulations which set forth the required contents for such notices and instruct registrants and auditors to notify the Office of the Chief Accountant within the applicable time periods. These reporting requirements should give auditors additional leverage to prompt management to correct illegal acts. Financial Reporting Release No. 49, Implementation of Section 10A of the Securities Exchange Act of 1934, 62 Fed. Reg. 12,743 (1997) (codified at 17 C.F.R. § 240.10A-1). Some commentators, however, fear that clients may become less candid with their auditors and that Section 10A may actually make financial statements less, and not more, effective.   *See, e.g.,* Dan L. Goldwasser, *The Private Securities Litigation Reform Act of 1995: Impact on Accountants,* CPA J., Jan. 1997, at 72, 75.

In February 1997, the ASB issued SAS No. 82, Consideration of Fraud in a Financial Statement Audit, which toughens auditing standards and requires auditors to assess specifically and document the risk that fraud may cause material misstatements in every audit.   In this context, fraud includes both intentional misrepresentations in financial statements, sometimes referred to as "cooking the books," and misappropriation or theft of assets.   The new SAS revises the third general standard of the ten basic standards, supersedes SAS No. 53, and requires other conforming changes to certain auditing standards and other materials, such as industry audit and accounting guides.   In particular, SAS No. 82 expands an auditor's responsibilities to plan and perform an audit to require that the auditor obtain reasonable assurance that neither error nor fraud has caused material misstatements in the financial statements.   The new pronouncement describes various frauds and accompanying characteristics, identifies factors that an auditor should consider in assessing the risk that fraud has caused material misstatements in the financial statements, and provides guidance about how the auditor should respond to the assessment's results.   In addition, the standard suggests how an auditor should evaluate test results as they relate to the possibility that fraud may cause material misstatements, requires the auditor to document the risk assessment and response, and finally reaffirms the requirement that the auditor inform management, the audit committee and perhaps government regulators about any material fraud that an audit detects.   The new rules apply to audits involving financial statements for periods ending on or after December 15, 1997. Consideration of Fraud in a Financial Statement Audit, Statement on Auditing Standards No. 82 (American Inst. of Certified Pub. Accountants 1997); Steve Burkholder, *New Fraud Reporting Rules Are Not Mere Clarification, ASB Chairman Warns,* 28 Sec. Reg. & L. Rep. (BNA) 1528 (1996); *see also* Jeanne Calderon & Rachel Kowal, *Auditors Whistle an Unhappy Tune,* 75 Denv. U.L. Rev. 419 (1998) (fearing that SAS No. 82 establishes a benchmark for alleging auditor fraud within the federal securities law context). Even under the new standard, a lawyer should remember that audits provide only reasonable assurance, not absolute assurance, that fraud has not caused a material misstatement in the financial statements.   As a result, even an audit conducted according to GAAS may not detect a material misstatement.

E. ALTERNATIVES TO AUDITS

1. REVIEW

Page 181. Insert the following at the beginning of this discussion:

Late in 1999, the SEC adopted new rules and amendments that require an independent public accountant to review a registrant's interim financial statements, using professional standards and procedures for conducting such reviews, before the registrant files its quarterly report with the Commission on either Form 10-Q or Form 10-QSB. If a registrant states that an independent public accountant has reviewed the interim financial statements, the registrant must file the accountant's report on the review with the interim financial statements. The provisions apply to quarterly reports for fiscal quarters ending on or after March 15, 2000. Audit Committee Disclosure, 64 Fed. Reg. 73,389 (1999) (amending 17 C.F.R. §§ 210.10-01(d), 228.310(b)).

F. PUBLISHED SOURCES OF GAAP, GAAS AND OTHER FINANCIAL INFORMATION

1. GAAP

Page 185. Insert the following in the list of helpful Internet sites:

IASC	http://www.iasc.org.uk
ISB	http://www.cpaindependence.org
IFAC	http://www.ifac.org

Page 185. At the end of the first full paragraph on this page, add the following:

The Tax and Accounting Sites Directory at <http://www.taxsites.com>, developed and maintained by Dennis Schmidt, a professor of accounting at the University of Northern Iowa, contains twelve subject headings for accounting sites and enables easy access to a variety of Web sites. Jan Davis Tudor, *More Magnificent Meta Sites*, CyberSkeptics Guide, Nov./Dec. 1997, at 4.

3. CURRENT DEVELOPMENTS

Page 186. At the end of the discussion under this heading add the following:

The AICPA's home page on the World Wide Web at <http://www.aicpa.org>, through the NewsFlash! link, allows law students and lawyers to view summaries of recent developments in the accounting and auditing fields.

4. General Financial Information

Page 187. At the end of the first paragraph add the following:

The SEC's EDGAR site on the Internet receives a million hits a day and probably ranks as the most popular government site on the Internet. *SEC Seeks to Modernize, Simplify Its Regulations*, Corp. Counsel Weekly, Nov. 18, 1998, at 7.

G. Accountants' Legal Liability

Page 187. After the third sentence, insert the following:

The trial judge later granted the firm's motion for a new trial. The court of appeals affirmed in part, reversed in part, and remanded the case for retrial on a single claim; the Supreme Court of Arizona denied further review. Standard Chartered PLC v. Price Waterhouse, 190 Ariz. 6, 945 P.2d 317 (1997).

Page 188. After the sentence that ends on the fifteenth line, insert the following:

In 1998, KPMG Peat Marwick agreed to pay $75 million to settle four lawsuits arising from Orange County's bankruptcy, substantially less than the $3.5 billion that the suits sought, including the county's $3 billion damage claim. In 1999, Ernst & Young agreed to pay a record $335 million to settle a class action lawsuit that shareholders of Cendant Corp. brought for alleged negligence in failing to detect widespread fraud at one of Cendant's predecessors and another $185 million to settle a lawsuit that sought $800 million in compensatory damages and $3 billion in punitive damages arising from the bankruptcy of Merry-Go-Round Enterprises Inc., a now-defunct clothing retailer. Vivien Lou Chen, *Ernst & Young to Pay $335 Million in Audit Lawsuit*, L.A. TIMES, Dec. 18, 1999, at C1; *Ernst & Young, Md. Concern Reach $185 Million Settlement*, 31 Sec. Reg. & L. Rep. (BNA) 583 (1999); *KPMG Peat Marwick Settles Orange County Lawsuits for $75 Million*, 30 Sec. Reg. & L. Rep. (BNA) 801 (1998).

Page 210. At the end of the first full paragraph, insert the following:

See generally Joyce Holley & Dannye Holley, *Auditor Common Law Liability in the State Courts: A Recent (1980-94) Outcome Restatement and Perspectives of the Accounting and Legal Professions*, 6 U. Miami Bus. L.J. 1 (1997) (analyzing almost fifty cases since 1980 and identifying unanswered questions concerning auditor common law liability). At least two recent cases have recognized comparative fault defenses in actions for negligent misrepresentations. *See, e.g.*, ESCA Corp. v. KPMG Peat Marwick, 86 Wash. App. 628, 939 P.2d 1228 (1997), petition for review granted,

133 Wash. 2d 1029, 950 P.2d 475 (1998) (based on state comparative negligence statute); Standard Chartered PLC v. Price Waterhouse, 190 Ariz. 6, 945 P.2d 317 (1997) (as corrected on denial of reconsideration) (based on both constitutional and statutory provisions). As an example of recent legislation affecting accountants' legal liability, Texas recently enacted a statute which limits the legal liability of accountants involved in issuing securities of small businesses to no more than three times their fees, provided that the accountant did not engage in intentional wrongdoing. 1997 Tex. Gen. Laws ch. 638, § 1 (codified at Tex. Rev. Civ. Stat. Ann. art. 581-33, subsec. N (West Supp. 1998). Other states have enacted privity statutes that raise often insurmountable obstacles to a third party's ability to maintain a professional liability action against an accountant. See, e.g., H. Keith Morrison & Robert W. George, *Arkansas's Privity Requirement for Attorney and Accountant Liability*, 51 Ark. L. Rev. 697, 705-11 (also discussing privity statutes in Illinois, Kansas, Utah and Michigan).

Page 210. At the end of the first note, insert the following:

Lewis D. Lowenfels & Alan R. Bromberg, *Liabilities of Lawyers and Accountants Under Rule 10b-5*, 53 BUS. LAW. 1157 (analyzing recent decisions involving accountants after Central Bank v. First Interstate Bank, 511 U.S. 164, 114 S.Ct. 1439, 128 L.Ed.2d 119 (1994), abolished aiding and abetting liability in certain private securities fraud actions).

H. INTERNAL CONTROL

Page 213. Insert the following at the end of the first paragraph:

In Staff Accounting Bulletin No. 99, the SEC staff recently reminded registrants that immaterial, but intentional misstatements can indeed violate the FCPA record-keeping and internal controls requirements. In addition to the factors that registrants and their lawyers should consider in evaluating materiality, the bulletin urges them to contemplate the significance of the misstatement, how the misstatement arose, the cost to correct the misstatement, and the clarity of accounting guidance addressing the misstatement in assessing whether the enterprise has kept accurate books, records and accounts in "reasonable detail." Materiality, Staff Accounting Bulletin No. 99, 64 Fed. Reg. 45,150 (1999), reprinted in 7 Fed. Sec. L. Rep. (CCH) ¶ 75,501, at 64,219-3 (Dec. 8, 1999).

Page 216. Insert the following at the beginning of note 1:

The SEC recently brought the first action in about a decade alleging a violation of the FCPA's foreign payments provision. The registrant consented, without admitting or denying the allegations, to a final judgment which permanently enjoined the company from violating the FCPA's books and records and internal controls requirements and ordered the company to pay a $300,000 penalty. The underlying complaint alleged that the company and several former officers and employees offered payments to Indonesian government employees to influence their decisions affecting a subsidiary's business and then concealed the payments by falsely documenting and recording the transactions as routine business expenses. SEC v. Triton Energy Corporation, Civil Action No. 1:97CV00401 (D.D.C. 1997), reported in Accounting and Auditing Enforcement Release No. 890, [1995-1998 Accounting and Auditing Enforcement Releases Transfer Binder] Fed. Sec. L. Rep. (CCH) ¶ 74,405. Various SEC officials have warned that they have started to see a resurgence in these kinds of cases as economic globalization increases. Phyllis A. Diamond, *Independence, Role in Ownership Issues Can Help Boards Avoid Liability, Delaware's Chief Justice Veasey Says*, Corp. Counsel Weekly, May 7, 1997, at 8.

Page 216. At the end of note 2, add the following:

In a recent speech at the Tenth Tulane Corporate Law Institute, SEC Chairman Arthur Levitt reminded directors on audit committees that they must oversee financial reporting and internal controls because they serve as the primary link between the directors and the outside auditors. In fulfilling this responsibility, Chairman Levitt urged the members of an audit committee to question the auditor about the quality of the enterprise's financial reporting to ensure that the shareholders get relevant and reliable financial information. *SEC 'Should Be More Outspoken' On Directors' Duty to Monitor Management*, 30 Sec. Reg. & L. Rep. (BNA) 398 (1998).

In possible contrast to the SEC's emphasis on audit committees, Professor Melvin A. Eisenberg, one of the leading scholars in corporate law today, suggests that, given the monitoring function that modern corporate law assigns to the board of directors, ultimate responsibility for internal control rests in the entire board and not only in the audit committee. Melvin A. Eisenberg, *The Board of Directors and Internal Control*, 19 Cardozo L. Rev. 237 (1997). Regardless of whether modern corporate law allows the board of directors to delegate this responsibility to an audit committee, internal control continues to grow in importance in contemporary corporate governance.

Page 218. At the end of note 4, insert the following:

Even more recently, the Best Practices Council of the National Association of Corporate Directors issued a report in March 1998 to highlight recent regulatory and legal developments, including the Private Securities Litigation Reform Act of 1995 and SAS No. 82, that increasingly compel businesses to focus on internal fraud detection. As basic principles in the "battle against fraud and other illegal activity," the report identifies setting the tone at the top through example and communication to create a clear policy against improper conduct, explicitly focusing on fraud risk, and developing an effective communication process between directors, officers, senior managers and employees. To implement such a framework, the council's suggestions include director education and involvement in legal developments and accounting pronouncements; broad equity ownership to encourage vested self-interest and commitment by directors, managers and employees; established processes to deter and detect fraud and other illegal activity; periodic assessment of fraud risks and monitoring of management's efforts to prevent fraud; an established process for responding to incidents involving fraud and other illegal activity; strong external audits; and regular board communication with external auditors. The council especially directed the report toward "fast growing 'entrepreneurial' companies that have not yet begun to focus on the threat of fraud and other illegal activity as the organization rapidly expands." National Association of Corporate Directors, Report of the NACD Best Practices Council: Coping With Fraud and Other Illegal Activity (1998).

Page 218. At the end of the first paragraph in note 5, insert the following citation:

Edward S. Adams & David E. Runkle, *The Easy Case for Derivatives Use: Advocating a Corporate Fiduciary Duty to Use Derivatives*, 41 WM. & MARY L. REV. 595, 600-15 (2000) (defining and describing four major categories of derivatives and explaining how and why enterprises use derivatives).

Page 219. At the end of the first paragraph, insert the following:

In 1998, Sumitomo Corp. agreed to pay a record $150 million to settle Commodity Futures Trading Commission market manipulation charges, approximately $8 million to close Financial Services Authority charges in London, $99 million to resolve civil market manipulation charges in the United States, and another $42.5 million to settle two antitrust class actions, arising from the unauthorized copper transactions. Donna Harris-Aiken, *Sumitomo Resolves Outstanding Class Actions By Agreeing to Settle Calif. Suits for $42.5M*, 30 Sec. Reg. & L. Rep. (BNA) 1412 (1998); *Sumitomo Agrees to Pay $99M To Settle N.Y. Actions Over Copper Trades*, 30 Sec. Reg. & L. Rep. (BNA) 1260 (1998); Donna Harris-Aikens, *Sumitomo Corp. To Pay Record $150 Million To Settle Charges of Market Manipulation*, 30 Sec. Reg. & L. Rep. (BNA) 760 (1998).

Page 219. Add the following citation at the end of the second paragraph:

Suzanne E. Bish, Note, *A Guide to Narrow the Derivatives' Understanding Gap and Reduce Losses: How to Increase Knowledge, Controls, and Reporting*, 58 Ohio St. L.J. 539 (1997) (suggesting that full disclosure, increased understanding and involvement by top management and the board of directors, consistent reporting, enhanced internal control systems, improved accounting and disclosure standards, and the use of an internal control letter as part of independent audits can avoid future financial disasters).

CHAPTER III

THE TIME VALUE OF MONEY

A. IMPORTANCE TO LAWYERS

Page 222. Insert the following after the first full sentence at the top of the page:

In *Atlantic Mutual Insurance Company v. Commissioner*, 523 U.S. 382, 118 S.Ct. 1413, 140 L.Ed.2d 542 (1998), an insurance tax case, for example, the Supreme Court observed that the relevant Internal Revenue Code provisions enabled the insurer to claim "a current deduction for future loss payments without adjusting for the 'time value of money'--the fact that "'[a] dollar today is worth more than a dollar tomorrow.'"" 523 U.S. at 384, 118 S.Ct. at 1415, 140 L.Ed.2d at 546 (quoting the casebook).

Page 222. Replace the first full paragraph with the following:

Although the time value of money has a long history in finance and accounting, financial accounting standards have traditionally ignored present value, using instead the undiscounted sum of estimated future cash flows for various purposes. In February 2000, however, the Financial Accounting Standards Board issued a new Statement of Financial Accounting Concepts that establishes a framework for using future cash flows, as discounted to present value, as the basis for certain accounting measurements. Using Cash Flow Information and Present Value in Accounting Measurements, Statement of Financial Accounting Concepts No. 7 (Financial Accounting Standards Bd. 2000). You may recall from the last chapter that Statements of Financial Accounting Concepts provide an overall framework as FASB sets accounting rules. As the Board issues new or revised accounting standards, the new concepts statement will likely increase significantly the importance of time value of money principles in financial accounting. Regardless of whether the new concepts statement significantly changes financial accounting, this chapter will acquaint you with the basics of time value analysis. By chapter's end, you will be able to analyze and resolve problems involving the time value of money.

B. INTEREST

1. FACTORS DETERMINING INTEREST RATES

Page 223. Add the following citation after the second sentence of the second paragraph:

See, e.g., Medcom Holding Co. v. Baxter Travenol Laboratories, Inc., 200 F.3d 518 (7th Cir. 2000) (concluding that the district court should have awarded prejudgment interest at a market rate rather than the statutory rate of five percent simple interest).

Page 223. Add the following citations at the end of the second paragraph:

Compare Gary R. Albrecht & John H. Wood, *Risk and Damage Awards: Short-Term Bonds Vs. Long-Term Bonds*, J. Leg. Econ., Spring/Summer 1997, at 48-49 (arguing that because individuals can minimize inflation risk by investing in short-term as opposed to long-term securities, courts should use short-term interest rates in present value computations) *with* Thomas R. Ireland, *The Pfeifer Decision, Risk and Damage Awards: An Extended Response to Albrecht and Wood*, J. Leg. Econ., Winter 1997/1998, at 23-24 (disagreeing with argument in previous article and suggesting that short-term bonds carry liquidity premiums rendering them unsuitable for use in setting discount rates in damage awards and that the new Treasury Inflation Indexed Securities (TIIS) that the U.S. Treasury recently began issuing offer a better mechanism for eliminating inflation uncertainty).

C. FUTURE VALUE

1. SINGLE AMOUNTS

c. PRACTICAL ADVICE: WHY YOU SHOULD START SAVING FOR YOUR RETIREMENT AS SOON AS POSSIBLE

Page 229. Replace the last two sentences of the first paragraph with the following:

From 1926 through 1999, according to Ibbotson Associates, a Chicago-based research firm, stocks in Standard & Poor's 500, an index which tracks 500 large companies and gauges the stock market's performance, have gained an average of 11.4 percent each year. Stocks in smaller companies have done even better, posting gains averaging 12.6 percent per year. Walter Updegrave, *Risk; Investors think the biggest risk they face with stocks is panicking and selling during short-term market meltdowns. They're wrong.*, MONEY, June 2000, at 133, 135; Philip Boroff, *NYSE*

Head Says Bubble Soon to be Dot-Gone, [Ft. Lauderdale] Sun-Sentinel, May 5, 2000, at 2D. During the period from 1926 through 1998, long-term government bonds have posted a 5.3 percent average annual return, short-term U.S. Treasury bills have earned a 3.8 percent average annual return, and inflation has averaged 3.1 percent per year. Jonathan Clements, *Dow 10,000? Prepare for the Hangover*, Wall St. J., Mar. 23, 1999, at C1; Dan Moreau, *Stocks Provide Best Long-Term Return*, Investor's Bus. Daily, Feb. 17, 1999, at B1.

CHAPTER IV

INTRODUCTION TO FINANCIAL STATEMENT ANALYSIS AND FINANCIAL RATIOS

A. IMPORTANCE TO LAWYERS

Page 252. Insert the following at the end of the second paragraph:

In *Weiner v. Quaker Oats Co.*, 129 F.3d 310 (3rd Cir. 1997), for example, the Third Circuit recently reinstated a securities fraud claim that alleged the defendant company and its chief executive officer had improperly failed to update a projected "guideline" for a debt-to-equity ratio that became inaccurate because the company's planned $1.7 billion, entirely debt-financed acquisition of Snapple Beverage Corp. would increase the debt-to-total capitalization ratio significantly above the previously articulated "'upper-60 percent range'" guideline to approximately eighty percent. See also *Weiner v. Quaker Oats Co.*, 1999 U.S. Dist. LEXIS 17222 (N.D. Ill. 1999) (granting plaintiffs' motion for class certification, certifying a class, and appointing class representatives in the same action).

C. THE BALANCE SHEET

1. CHANGES IN OWNERS' EQUITY

Page 261. Replace the second full paragraph with the following:

In fact, the FASB recently adopted new accounting rules that recognize that the change in net assets between successive balance sheets can effectively measure an enterprise's financial performance. In 1997, the FASB issued Statement of Financial Accounting Standards No. 130, Reporting Comprehensive Income, which applies to fiscal years beginning after December 15, 1997. In essence, the new pronouncement requires enterprises to report the net changes in their equity from all transactions other than with owners during a period in the financial statements and to display this so-called "comprehensive income" and its components with the same prominence as other financial statements. FASB Statement No. 130 describes "comprehensive income" as the change in an enterprise's net assets, or owners' equity, during a period from transactions and other events and circumstances from nonowner sources. The term, therefore, includes all increases and decreases in net assets during the period except those changes resulting from investments by and distributions to owners. Reporting Comprehensive Income, Statement of Financial Accounting additional note after the *In re Reliance Group Holdings, Inc.* case that appears on pages 377-81 of the casebook and in the materials on "Income Statement Presentation and Disclosure" on pages 481-84.

2. ANALYTICAL TERMS AND RATIOS

b. FINANCIAL RATIOS

(2) Leverage Ratios

a) DEBT TO EQUITY

Page 265. At the end of this section, insert the following paragraph:

The September 1998 financial crisis involving Long-Term Capital Management L.P. ("LTCM") illustrates both the debt to equity ratio and the danger of excessive leverage. Then chairperson of the Commodity Futures Trading Commission Brooksley Born told an audience at the Chicago-Kent College of Law Derivatives and Commodities Law Institute that, by the time of its near collapse, LTCM had borrowed approximately 100 times its capital. Such borrowings would translate to a debt-equity ratio of 100-to-1. More than a month later, when responding to press reports that she and the Commission had kept silent about certain information that might have revealed LTCM's problems before they became public, Chairperson Born stated that the year-end 1997 financial statement that LTCM filed on March 16, 1998 did not show abnormal leverage. She explained that LTCM's annual statements showed a 25-to-1 assets-to-capital ratio, well within the normal range for a financial services company. She noted that the ratios for other investment houses, such as Donaldson, Lufkin & Jenrette, exceeded 30-to-1. Only a $3.6 billion emergency bailout by various top financial institutions that the New York Federal Reserve Bank helped arrange avoided LTCM's complete collapse. Donna Harris-Aikens, *Born Says CFTC Had No Prior Information Forewarning of Hedge Fund's Financial Woes*, 30 Sec. Reg. & L. Rep. (BNA) 1668 (1998); Michael Bologna, *LTCM Crisis Shows Need for Better Controls Over OTC Derivatives Markets, Born Says*, 30 Sec. Reg. & L. Rep. (BNA) 1514 (1998).

D. THE INCOME STATEMENT

2. RATIO ANALYSIS

b. PROFITABILITY RATIOS

(1) Earnings Per Share

Page 272. Replace the last four sentences in the last paragraph with the following discussion that reflects the issuance of FASB Statement No. 128 which simplifies the rules for computing earnings per share for financial periods ending after December 15, 1997:

In a collaborative effort with the International Accounting Standards Committee, the FASB recently issued Statement of Financial Accounting Standards No. 128, Earnings per Share, to simplify the standards for computing earnings per share and to conform the applicable rules more closely to international accounting standards. The pronouncement requires enterprises with publicly held common stock, or with outstanding contractual obligations that could allow holders to obtain common stock either during, or after the end of, the reporting period, to report figures for *basic earnings per share* and, if applicable, *diluted earnings per share.* The new terms "basic earnings per share" and "diluted earnings per share" replace the previously used labels "primary earnings per share" and "fully diluted earnings per share," respectively. Under the new rules, *basic earnings per share* describes the amount of earnings for the period available to each share of common stock outstanding during the period. An enterprise computes basic earnings per share by dividing income available to common shareholders by the weighted average of common shares outstanding during the period. FASB Statement No. 128 defines *diluted earnings per share* as the amount of earnings for the period available to each share of common stock outstanding during the period and to each share that would have been outstanding, assuming that the enterprise issued common shares for all dilutive potential common shares outstanding during the period. *Dilutive potential common shares,* such as options, warrants and convertible securities, give the holder the right to acquire common shares either during, or after the end of, the reporting period and would reduce the earnings per share if the enterprise had issued the necessary common shares to the holder. Computing diluted earnings per share can present quite a challenge, so we will ignore the actual mechanics. The new rules apply to financial statements for periods ending after December 15, 1997. Earnings per Share, Statement of Financial Accounting Standards No. 128 (Financial Accounting Standards Bd. 1997). *See* Steve Burkholder, *Earnings Per Share Standards Issued by Global Rulemakers, FASB,* 29 Sec. Reg. & L. Rep. (BNA) 321 (1997).

F. MANAGEMENT'S DISCUSSION AND ANALYSIS

1. THE PURPOSE OF REQUIRED DISCLOSURE IN MD&A

Page 289. At the end of note 2 at the top of the page, add the following:

The National Investor Relations Institute recently released its "1998 Study of Corporate Disclosure" which found that the number of companies willing to include projections or other soft information in their filings with the Securities and Exchange Commission has increased from fifty percent in 1995 to sixty-seven percent in 1998. As a result, the Institute concluded that the evidence strongly suggests that the safe harbors for forward-looking statements are working. *NIRI Survey Finds Improved Disclosure of Soft Info in News Releases, SEC Filings*, 30 Sec. Reg. & L. Rep. (BNA) 896 (1998). In addition, the Securities Litigation Uniform Standards Act of 1998, Pub. L. No. 105-353, § 101, 112 Stat. 3227, closed a loophole in the Private Securities Litigation Reform Act of 1995 that otherwise might have allowed plaintiffs to avoid the federal safe harbors and to file suits based on state securities law standards. The legislation requires plaintiffs to bring class actions involving nationally traded securities in federal court under uniform federal standards. *President Signs Uniform Standards Bill, Sees Investor Benefit, Fewer Frivolous Suits*, 30 Sec. Reg. & L. Rep. (BNA) 1602 (1998).

3. A recent study finds evidence that firms that financial analysts rate favorably for disclosure quality enjoy lower effective interest costs when issuing debt. This finding supports the argument that timely, accurate and detailed disclosures reduce investors' risks and the cost of capital. Partha Sengupta, *Corporate Disclosure Quality and the Cost of Debt*, 73 Acct. Rev. 459 (1998).

2. COMPLIANCE WITH GAAP ALONE DOES NOT SATISFY MD&A REQUIREMENTS

Page 295. Replace note 2 at the top of the page with the following:

2. The SEC has pursued at least two other MD&A cases involving registrants that did not violate GAAP. In 1994, the SEC instituted administrative proceedings against a registrant for failing to disclose a material slowdown in sales in its periodic filings, even though the corporation had disclosed the information in a press release. In re Shared Medical Systems Corp., Exchange Act Release No. 33632, 1994 WL 49960 (S.E.C.) (February 17, 1994). The SEC concluded that a registrant must disclose known trends in the MD&A section, even though the registrant has previously announced the trends to the public elsewhere.

More recently, Sony Corporation ("Sony") settled administrative charges arising from the company's failure to disclose losses in its Sony Pictures Entertainment Inc.

subsidiary ("SPE") in the MD&A sections of its annual reports for the fiscal year ended March 31, 1994 and two other current reports that the company filed on Form 6-K, the document that foreign issuers use to file reports of material information with the SEC. These inadequate disclosures occurred during the several months before Sony wrote down about $2.7 billion in goodwill related to SPE's acquisition. Despite the expressed preference of its outside auditors and own financial officers, Sony did not report the results of SPE as a separate industry segment. Instead, the company reported the combined results of SPE and Sony's profitable music business as a single "entertainment" segment. This treatment obscured the approximately $967 million in net losses that SPE had incurred after the acquisition and before the close of the fiscal year ended March 31, 1994, which the SEC described as a "known trend." In addition, Sony's filings failed to disclose that the company had been considering the possible need to write down a substantial part of the goodwill attributable to SPE for more than a year.

As part of the settlement, Sony agreed to engage an independent auditor to examine its MD&A presentation for the fiscal year ending March 31, 1999 and to adopt procedures to ensure that its new chief financial officer assumes primary responsibility for ensuring that the company's disclosures comply with legal and accounting requirements. In March 1998, the AICPA issued standards setting forth the procedures that an auditor should undertake when examining a registrant's MD&A in such an engagement. In a related civil action, Sony also agreed to pay a $1 million civil penalty, an amount which equals the largest sum the SEC has ever received for a non-antifraud violation, without admitting or denying wrongdoing. In re Sony Corporation, Accounting and Auditing Enforcement Release No. 1061, 1998 WL 439898 (S.E.C.) (Aug. 5, 1998); see also Sony Settles Disclosure Charges Over Losses by Movie Subsidiary, 30 Sec. Reg. & L. Rep. (BNA) 1203 (1998).

Because the SEC has not pursued any other similar cases, the effects of the Caterpillar, Shared Medical Systems, and Sony Corporation matters remain unclear. Nevertheless, those administrative proceedings document the importance that the SEC places on MD&A and highlight the types of prospective information that a reader can expect to find in MD&A in the future.

3. ENFORCEMENT ISSUES ARISING FROM LIQUIDITY PROBLEMS

Page 299. Insert the following discussion, problem and new section after the note on the bottom of the page:

More recently, the SEC brought separate public administrative proceedings against Terex Corporation ("Terex"), its former chairman, and an affiliate and against two former officers in the corporate group, for inadequately disclosing an accounting adjustment and its effect on the current liabilities of Terex and Fruehauf Trailer Corporation ("Fruehauf"). The accounting adjustment caused Fruehauf to fail to meet specified financial ratios in long-term loans totaling $82.7 million from various financial institutions and to violate certain loan covenants, which gave the lenders the right to accelerate the loans. In such circumstances, FASB Statement No. 78, "Classification of Obligations that are Callable by the Creditor," requires that the borrower reclassify the underlying long-term obligation as a current liability. Because Fruehauf continued to classify the $82.7 million as long-term liabilities, both Fruehauf and its ultimate parent, Terex, understated their current liabilities. In re Terex Corp., Accounting and Auditing Enforcement Release No. 1126, 7 Fed. Sec. L. Rep. (CCH) ¶ 74,633, 1999 WL 228423 (1999); In re Skaff, Accounting and Auditing Enforcement Release No. 1127, 7 Fed. Sec. L. Rep. (CCH) ¶ 74,634, 1999 WL 228426 (1999).

PROBLEM

Problem 4.4. Locate Ben & Jerry's MD&As for the fiscal years ending December 30, 1995, December 26, 1998 and December 25, 1999 and for the most recent fiscal period. You can obtain this information from EDGAR at <http://www.sec.gov>, via the "Financial Info" link under the "Company Info" heading on Ben & Jerry's home page at <http://www.benjerry.com>, or by using LEXIS® • NEXIS® or WESTLAW®. You can also find excerpts from Ben & Jerry's 1999 Form 10-K in the appendix to this supplement. Do you find anything in the 1992, 1995, 1998, 1999 or more recent MD&As that suggests the onset of the problems which Ben & Jerry's has encountered, any recovery, or the prospects for the future? Explain briefly.

G. THE FUTURE OF FINANCIAL AND NON-FINANCIAL REPORTING

Increasingly, analysts and other financial statement users have criticized the current financial accounting model, which generally uses historical cost to present quantitative information, as irrelevant to many investment, credit and other decisions. In addition to taking initial steps toward a fair value-based system, which could eventually require enterprises to report all financial assets and liabilities at fair value, *supra* at 1-2, the FASB decided in early 1998 to undertake a research effort that could lead to a framework for a new business reporting model. The Business Reporting Research Project, which the FASB expects to complete in September 2000, will examine current corporate disclosure practices and identify those practices and non-quantitative information that might enhance the data already contained in financial statements. For example, an enterprise might disclose key trends in operating or performance data and management's analysis of changes in such data, forward-looking information about such things as opportunities, risks and management's plans, or information about order backlogs, customer satisfaction, management, ownership, and intangible assets, especially those not currently included in financial statements. The effort seeks to develop a framework for the types of supplemental and non-financial information that enterprises should provide to investors. The project arises in large part in response to a 1994 report of the

AICPA's Special Committee on Financial Reporting, which FASB Chairman Edmund Jenkins headed, and an earlier 1993 report from the Association for Investment Management and Research, a leading group of financial statement users. Steve Burkholder, *New Business Reporting Model Talks Center on Risk of Competitive Harm*, 30 Sec. Reg. & L. Rep. (BNA) 1621 (1998); Steve Burkholder, *With Naming of Panel Chair, FASB Plans Effort on New Business Reporting Model*, 30 Sec. Reg. & L. Rep. (BNA) 504 (1998); Steve Burkholder, *FASB in 'Very Good' State, Jenkins Says; Baker Bill Casts Shadow*, 30 Sec. Reg. & L. Rep. (BNA) 251, 252 (1998); *see also* Richard I. Miller & Michael R. Young, *Financial Reporting and Risk Management in the 21st Century*, 65 Fordham L. Rev. 1987 (1997) (discussing the potential liability arising from improvements in financial reporting systems, which would presumably move away from objectively verifiable data and towards more subjective information, which in turn would increase the opportunity for second-guessing and the enterprise's exposure to litigation, and how individuals and organizations responsible for structuring financial reporting relationships can manage that liability both to facilitate honest financial reporting and to give financial reporting systems the flexibility to evolve).

CHAPTER V

LEGAL ISSUES INVOLVING SHAREHOLDERS' EQUITY AND THE BALANCE SHEET

B. LIMITATIONS ON THE ISSUANCE OF SHARES

Page 306. Add the following citation at the end of the first sentence to note 2 at the bottom of the page:

See, e.g., Torres v. Speiser, 701 N.Y.S.2d 360 (N.Y. App. Div. 2000) (holding that Business Corporation Law § 504, which prohibits a corporation's initial issuance of shares for less than par value or before the purchaser has paid the full purchase price, does not apply to a resale of shares among shareholders).

C. DISTRIBUTIONS AND LEGAL RESTRICTIONS

1. DIVIDENDS AND REDEMPTIONS

Page 309. Replace the first full sentence at the top of the page with the following:

After the Taxpayer Relief Act of 1997 and the more recently enacted IRS Restructuring and Reform Act of 1998, if the shareholder owned the shares for more than one year the gain can qualify for capital gains treatment, which means that an individual will pay tax on the gain at a statutory rate of no more than twenty percent.

2. STOCK DIVIDENDS AND STOCK SPLITS

Page 315. At the end of the first full paragraph, insert the following:

As more and more states move toward the MBCA's approach to eliminate the distinction between stock dividends and stock splits, two commentators recently concluded, based upon an empirical study, that the legal capital system's statutory restrictions on stock dividends enhance management's ability to use stock distributions to communicate with shareholders. The commentators found that price increases following the announcement of a large stock distribution effected as a stock dividend exceeded the price increases following a stock split. The article contends that the choice of accounting treatment for stock distributions necessary under the legal capital system enables management to signal its expectations about the firm's future success or failure because that choice affects the company's ability to pay cash dividends in the future. The commentators argue that policymakers should take care that corporate law reforms to the legal capital system do not hinder the flow of information to investors. Craig A. Peterson & Norman W. Hawker, *Does Corporate Law Matter? Legal Capital Restrictions on Stock Distributions*, 31 Akron L. Rev. 175 (1997).

3. RESTRICTIONS ON CORPORATE DISTRIBUTIONS

a. STATUTORY RESTRICTIONS

(1) Corporate Law

Page 316. After the citation following the first sentence under this heading, insert the following:

In addition, the courts in some states have invalidated transactions or refused to enforce agreements that violate the statutory restrictions on distributions. *Compare* McAlister v. Peregrine Enterprises, Inc., 1997 WL 746373 (Tenn. App. 1997) (accepting the corporate defendant's argument that the redemption of plaintiff's stock could violate the Tennessee statute that governs distributions to shareholders, reversing a grant of summary judgment for plaintiff, and remanding the case for further proceedings) *with* Minnelusa Co. v. Andrikopoulos, 929 P.2d 1321 (Colo. 1996) (adopting the majority view among state appellate courts refusing to allow the redeeming corporation to challenge a repurchase's validity on the grounds that the repurchase violated statutory prohibitions and holding that neither the defendant corporation nor the individual shareholder that guaranteed the underlying promissory notes could use the Florida stock repurchase statute to void their obligations under a stock repurchase agreement).

a) SURPLUS STATUTES

(i) Any Surplus

Page 318. In the only full paragraph, delete the two references to New York law and the related citation. Effective February 22, 1998, New York repealed section 510(c) of its Business Corporation Law, which previously required corporations making distributions from capital surplus to provide written notice of that fact to any shareholder receiving the distribution. N.Y. Bus. Corp. Law § 510 (McKinney Supp. 1998).

(3) Relationship of GAAP to Statutory Restrictions

Page 334. A recent decision of the Supreme Court of Delaware discussed below held that the board of directors can revalue assets and liabilities, and therefore can legitimately depart from the balance sheet, before concluding that a redemption did not unlawfully impair capital under Delaware law. In addition, and effective February 22, 1998, New York repealed section 102(a)(2) and (6) of its Business Corporation Law, which had previously defined "[c]apital surplus" and "[e]arned surplus." N.Y. Bus. Corp. Law § 102 (Supp. 1998). As a result of these developments, in the first full paragraph in Note 1 delete everything after the first two sentences and substitute the following:

More recently, the Supreme Court of Delaware expressly adhered to principles that allow a corporation to revalue assets and liabilities for purposes of determining whether the corporation can lawfully redeem shares. *Klang v. Smith's Food & Drug Centers, Inc.,* 702 A.2d 150, 154 (Del. 1997). In the unanimous opinion, Chief Justice Veasey wrote: "Balance sheets are not, however, conclusive indicators of surplus or a lack thereof." *Id.* at 152. Anticipating such revaluations, the corporate statutes in at least six states, Arkansas, Louisiana, Nevada, Ohio, Pennsylvania and Rhode Island, specifically address unrealized appreciation. *See, e.g.,* Ohio Rev. Code Ann. § 1701.32 (B) (Anderson 1992) (treating unrealized appreciation as capital surplus); R.I. Gen. Laws § 7-1.1-2(13) (providing that capital surplus, and not earned surplus, may include surplus arising from the good faith revaluations of assets).

Page 335. As a result of the recent amendments to New York corporate law described above, replace the second and third to the last sentences in the first full paragraph with the following:

You may recall that in three states, Louisiana, Missouri and Ohio, corporations making distributions from capital surplus must disclose that fact to the shareholders receiving the distribution. Ohio law specifically requires corporations to treat any surplus arising from unrealized appreciation as capital surplus. Ohio Rev. Code Ann. § 1701.32(B) (Anderson 1992).

Page 335. Replace the third and fourth sentences in note 3 with the following:

If so, would Ohio law require a reduction in earned surplus or capital surplus? You will recall from the previous discussion in note 1 that Ohio law specifically requires corporations to treat any surplus arising from unrealized appreciation as capital surplus.

Page 340. At the end of the first full paragraph, insert the following citation:

See also In re Inamed Corp., Accounting and Auditing Enforcement Release No. 1154, 7 Fed. Sec. L. Rep. (CCH) ¶ 74,661 (1999) (registrant consented to cease-and-desist order for, among other things, failing to recognize accrued expenses related to the waiver of an indenture covenants).

D. DRAFTING AND NEGOTIATING AGREEMENTS AND LEGAL DOCUMENTS CONTAINING ACCOUNTING TERMINOLOGY AND CONCEPTS

Page 360. Insert the following as note 1A:

1A. Given the devastating effects that changes in accounting principles can cause in restrictive covenants and other legal documents, lawyers should try to stay abreast of FASB's agenda. In that regard, we highlight several recent developments and areas to watch that potentially affect topics covered in the first five chapters.

(a) *Derivatives.* In 1998, the FASB completed its long-running project on derivatives, or financial contracts that derive their value from some underlying asset, and issued FASB Statement No. 133, Accounting for Derivative Instruments and Hedging Activities, originally effective for all quarters of fiscal years beginning after June 15, 1999. In June 1999, however, the FASB delayed the statement's effective date by one year. For companies using the calendar year for financial reporting, the rules will take effect on January 1, 2001. Accounting for Derivative Instruments and Hedging Activities–Deferral of the Effective Date of FASB Statement No. 133–an amendment of FASB Statement No. 133, Statement of Financial Accounting Standards No. 137 (Financial Accounting Standards Bd. 1999). When effective, FASB Statement No. 133 will require enterprises to show all derivatives as either assets or liabilities on the balance sheet, to measure those instruments at fair value, and to include the changes in those fair values during a period in earnings as either gains or losses. Before this pronouncement, literally trillions of dollars of derivatives contracts and changes in the value of those contracts did not appear in financial statements. Recent testimony before the Senate Agriculture Committee estimated the notional value of over-the-counter derivatives markets at $80 trillion in 1998. Merrill Goozner, *Regulators Back Derivatives Deregulation; Exchanges Also Ask Senate For Level Playing Field*, Chi. Trib., Feb. 11, 2000 at B1. In public statements about the recent financial crisis involving Long-Term Capital Management L.P. ("LTCM"), then chairperson of the Commodity Futures Trading Commission Brooksley Born has noted that at the time of its near collapse, LTCM held derivative positions with a notional value of $1.25 trillion, more than 1,000 times the firm's capital and significantly greater than its debt-equity ratio of 100-to-1. Michael Bologna, *LTCM Crisis Shows Need for Better Controls Over OTC Derivatives Markets, Born Says*, 30 Sec. Reg. & L. Rep. (BNA) 1514 (1998). Including amounts for these derivatives and their changes in value in financial statements obviously affects numerous financial ratios and could potentially cause, or cure, defaults in many contracts and lending agreements.

(b) *International accounting principles.* At what point in time will international accounting standards become acceptable in the United States? Will they ever become controlling in the United States? You may recall that FASB recently released the second edition of a special report that compares GAAP in the United States and international accounting standards. Financial Accounting Standards Board, The IASC-U.S. Comparison Project: A Report on the Similarities and Differences between IASC Standards and U.S. GAAP (2d ed. 1999). Although many of the variations between U.S. GAAP and IASC standards do not qualify as major and on-going developments will continue to eliminate or reduce other deviations, significant differences in recognition and measurement standards, the presence of choices or alternatives in both U.S. and IASC accounting principles, and lack of specific guidance in certain areas continue to exist. In addition, the almost certain likelihood that the industrialized world will soon embrace some system of global accounting standards warrants serious consideration, especially when drafting and negotiating agreements involving enterprises interested in cross-border securities listings.

(c) *Distinguishing liabilities and equity.* Some financial instruments, commonly referred to as *hybrid instruments*, contain both debt and equity characteristics. For example, mandatorily redeemable preferred shares obligate the issuer to repurchase the shares at particular times or under certain conditions. The FASB has tentatively adopted an approach that would treat a greater number of such hybrid instruments as liabilities, rather than as equity, the more typical result under current accounting principles. The board plans to issue a proposed standard on distinguishing between liabilities and equity as early as the 2000 third quarter. Again, any reclassifications that the new rules may potentially require could affect the leverage and coverage ratios commonly contained in loan agreements and other contracts.

(d) *Time value of money.* Although unlikely to produce as significant effects in the near future as the first two developments, the FASB recently issued a new concepts statement that sets forth discounted future cash flows and present value as the basis for various accounting measurements. See *supra* at 41. The concepts statement will presumably eventually lead to new or revised accounting standards that would modify the amounts at which various assets and liabilities appear on the balance sheet and establish rules for how changes in those amounts would affect the financial statements.

(e) *Financial instruments.* In recent years, the FASB has been gradually moving away from the so-called mixed-attribute accounting model that generally uses historical cost to an across-the-board fair value-based alternative, which would require enterprises to report all financial assets and liabilities at fair value. The concepts statement referred to in the previous paragraph could eventually lead to new or revised accounting standards that could significantly change financial reporting. Once again, fair value accounting--although almost certain to create a major controversy and admittedly at least several more years down the road--could significantly affect many financial ratios and, indeed, the entire framework for financial accounting.

We will identify other recent and potential developments potentially affecting contractual agreements and other legal documents in later chapters.

CHAPTER VI

REVENUE RECOGNITION AND ISSUES INVOLVING THE INCOME STATEMENT

A. IMPORTANCE TO LAWYERS

Page 366. At the end of the third full paragraph, insert the following:

Third, as a result of a recent accounting pronouncement and a related auditing interpretation, business enterprises and their auditors sometimes ask commercial lawyers, especially those specializing in bankruptcy issues, to give legal opinions that the transferor in a particular transaction has surrendered control, even though the transferor retains some continuing involvement either with the transferred asset or with the transferee, so that the parties can treat the transaction's substance as a "true sale" of all or part of the asset for financial accounting purposes.

Between 1997 and early 2000, dozens of public companies have announced major financial frauds, including improper revenue recognition practices at Cendant Corp., Informix Corp., Livent Inc., McKesson HBOC Inc., Mercury Finance Co., Centennial Technologies Inc., and Sunbeam Corp. *See, e.g., SEC Files 30 Enforcement Actions Targeting Financial Reporting Misdeeds*, 31 Sec. Reg. & L. Rep. (BNA) 1314 (1999) (describing actions against sixty-eight individuals and companies for alleged fraudulent financial reporting affecting fifteen different public companies); Elizabeth MacDonald, *SEC Holds Meetings to Discuss Accounting Woes*, Wall St. J., Aug. 12, 1998, at A2 (listing fifteen companies with reported bookkeeping snafus and discussing meetings where the SEC plans to explore accounting problems, including prematurely recording revenues and improperly deferring expenses). A recent SEC staff accounting bulletin notes that a March 1999 report entitled "Fraudulent Financial Reporting: 1987-1997 An Analysis of U.S. Public Companies" determined that more than half of the financial reporting frauds in the study involved overstating revenues. Revenue Recognition in Financial Statements, Staff Accounting Bulletin No. 101, 64 Fed. Reg. 1,122,290 (1999), reprinted in 7 Fed. Sec. Reg. L. Rep. (CCH) ¶ 75,565 (Apr. 12, 2000). Interestingly, numerous commentators have recently quipped that while revenues typically represent the largest item on the income statement, the smallest amount of accounting rules govern that item. *See, e.g.*, Elizabeth MacDonald, *Concerns on Internet Firms' Accounting Prompt SEC to Seek Tighter Standards*, Wall St. J., Nov. 18, 1999, at A4 (attributing the statement to SEC Chief Accountant Lynn Turner).

In 1998, SEC Chairman Arthur Levitt repeatedly highlighted "'a gradual, but noticeable erosion in the quality of financial reporting,'" and the SEC launched several major initiatives to remedy widespread problems in revenue recognition and financial accounting reporting. *See, e.g., Levitt Renews Call for Partnership To Bring About 'Cultural Change,'* 30 Sec. Reg. & L. Rep. (BNA) 1762 (1998); Steve Burkholder, *Levitt Seeks Corporate Help in SEC Drive To Stem 'Erosion' in Financial Reporting*, 30 Sec. Reg. & L. Rep. (BNA) 1674 (1998). In 1999, the SEC fined the former general counsel of Livent Inc. $25,000 and barred him from appearing or practicing before the SEC as an attorney for five years for his role in drafting and finalizing agreements related to a financial fraud and then concealing those agreements from the company's independent auditors). SEC v. Banks, Accounting and Auditing Enforcement Release No. 1153, 7 Fed. Sec. L. Rep. (CCH) ¶ 74,660 (1999).

The litigation that follows from financial frauds can impose enormous financial costs. To settle the class action securities fraud lawsuit that arose from Cendant's accounting irregularities, the company agreed to pay at least $2.38 billion, the largest settlement in the history of class action securities fraud litigation. *Cendant Corp. Agrees to Record Payment To Settle Class Financial Fraud Allegations*, 31 Sec. Reg. & L. Rep. (BNA) 1618 (1999).

B. ESSENTIAL REQUIREMENTS FOR REVENUE RECOGNITION

Page 367. After the third sentence in the first paragraph, insert the following citation as an example of a decision that implies that an exchange transaction has not occurred until the "seller" has received cash or a cash equivalent:

See, e.g., Stevelman v. Alias Research Inc., 174 F.3d 79, 83 (2d Cir. 1999) ("Industry standards and generally accepted accounting principles ('GAAP') require that a company's revenues not be recorded until such time as an *exchange* of merchandise has taken place and collection of the sales price on that merchandise is reasonably assured.") (emphasis in original).

Page 367. After the first paragraph, insert the following:

In Staff Accounting Bulletin No. 101, Revenue Recognition in Financial Statements, the SEC's staff recently attempted to put together all the authoritative literature found in various standards on revenue recognition in a single document. Perhaps more significantly, the staff expressed its belief that enterprises can recognize revenue only upon satisfying the following four conditions: (1) the evidence must persuasively demonstrate that an arrangement exists; (2) the enterprise must have delivered the product or performed the services; (3) the arrangement must contain a fixed or determinable sales price; and (4) the circumstances must reasonably assure collectibility. Revenue Recognition in Financial Statements, Staff Accounting Bulletin No. 101, 64 Fed. Reg. 1,122,290 (1999), reprinted in 7 Fed. Sec.

Reg. L. Rep. (CCH) ¶ ¶ 75,735, 75,761, at 64,341-42 (Jan. 12, 2000), 64,421-34 (Dec. 15, 1999 & Apr. 12, 2000); *see also* Revenue Recognition in Financial Statements, Staff Accounting Bulletin No. 101A, Amendment: Revenue Recognition in Financial Statements, 65 Fed. Reg. 16,811 (2000), reprinted in 7 Fed. Sec. Reg. L. Rep. (CCH) ¶ 75,761 at 64,432-34 (Dec. 15, 1999 & Apr. 12, 2000).

Page 373. Replace note 1 with the following:

1. A jury convicted two former officers of KAI on criminal charges arising from the scheme and acquitted a third ex-officer. A fourth former officer pled guilty and testified at trial pursuant to a cooperation agreement with the government. Following their convictions, the District Court sentenced the two former officers to federal prison terms of thirty-three and eighteen months, respectively, and an additional two years' probation upon release from prison. In addition, the District Court ordered Bernard F. Bradstreet, KAI's former president and chief financial officer, to pay $2.3 million in restitution and to disgorge an $80,000 unlawful bonus, plus prejudgment interest. United States v. Bradstreet, Accounting and Auditing Enforcement Release No. 865, 7 Fed. Sec. L. Rep. (CCH) ¶ 74,380 (1996); SEC v. Bradstreet, Accounting and Auditing Enforcement Release No. 824, 7 Fed. Sec. L. Rep. (CCH) ¶ 74,339 (1996); see also United States v. Bradstreet, 135 F.3d 46 (1st Cir.), cert. denied, 523 U.S. 1122, 118 S.Ct. 1805, 140 L.Ed.2d 944 (1998) (affirming convictions, but vacating the judgment because the District Court abused its discretion in granting a downward departure from the federal sentencing guidelines, and remanding for resentencing).

Page 373. After the second sentence in note 2, insert the following:

A higher market price may enable an enterprise to use overvalued ownership interests as "currency" in corporate acquisitions. *See, e.g.,* In re Horizon/CMS Healthcare Corporation Securities Litigation, 3 F. Supp. 1208, 1210 (1998). Management's desire to obtain a loan or more credit can also provide motivation for prematurely recognizing revenue and overstating accounts receivable. *See, e.g.,* SEC v. Adoni, 60 F. Supp. 2d 401 (D.N.J. 1999).

Page 374. At the end of note 3, insert the following:

Walter Schuetze, chief accountant at the SEC's Division of Enforcement has repeatedly stated that "premature revenue recognition remains 'the recipe of choice for cooking a company's books.'" Phyllis Diamond, *Accounting Fraud Is Top Priority, Enforcement Officials Tell CPAs*, 30 Sec. Reg. & L. Rep. (BNA) 1757 (1998); *see also* Steve Burkholder, *In Report, COSO Suggests Regulators, Exchanges Rethink Small Firm Exemptions*, 31 Sec. Reg. & L. Rep. (BNA) 448 (1999).

Page 374. After the first sentence in note 4, insert the following:

Lawyers that do not recognize "red flags" can easily find themselves participating in financial frauds and subject to disciplinary action. *See, e.g.*, SEC v. Banks, Accounting and Auditing Enforcement Release No. 1153, 7 Fed. Sec. L. Rep. (CCH) ¶ 74,660 (1999) (fining former general counsel of Livent Inc. $25,000 and barring him from appearing or practicing before the SEC as an attorney for five years for drafting and finalizing side agreements that required Livent to pay back amounts that the company improperly recognized as revenue and concealing those agreements from the company's independent auditors).

Page 374. Add the following at the end of the first paragraph in note 4:

In another case, the false entries in the general ledger included only dollar amounts and omitted the detailed information required and contained in legitimate journal entries. Miller v. Material Sciences Corp., 9 F. Supp. 2d 925, 928 (N.D. Ill. 1998). In yet another recent case, insiders referred to the lax accounting standards that the company's chief executive officer, Ernest Grendi, implemented and mandated as ""EGAAP," an acronym for Ernest Grendi's Accepted Accounting Practices."' AUSA Life Ins. Co. v. Ernst & Young, 206 F.3d 202 (2d Cir. 2000) (quoting the district court's opinion).

Pages 374-375. Delete note 6 and insert the following:

Financial statement users typically rely on financial statements to measure current income and to help predict future earnings. Analysts generally feel more comfortable predicting future results when a business's "bottom line" has increased, and should continue to grow, at a steady rate. Indeed, the stock markets have historically given higher price-earnings ratios to companies, such as General Electric Company and, until recently, The Coca-Cola Company, that have shown an ability to report steady, predictable earnings growth. Many business executives have been far too willing to accommodate investors' desires for steady growth and see nothing wrong with the practice. In this regard, the financial community often refers to managerial actions which increase or decrease a business's current reported earnings without generating a corresponding increase or decrease in the unit's long-term economic profitability as *earnings management* or *income smoothing*. The latter term refers to efforts to keep the business growing at a steady rate. When business executives manage or smooth earnings so that financial statements do not accurately reflect the enterprise's economic health and do not disclose these actions, they violate the trust which users place in financial statements and may cause users to reach decisions different from those that they might have made if they had enjoyed access to all relevant information. Understood in this context, earnings management and income smoothing raise important issues involving business and legal ethics.

The following speech by SEC Chairman Arthur Levitt identifies certain problem areas in current financial accounting and reporting, and sets forth an action plan to address the problems:

"The 'Numbers Game,'"
remarks by Arthur Levitt

Chairman, Securities and Exchange Commission
NYU Center for Law and Business, September 28, 1998.
(available at <http://www.sec.gov/news/speeches/spch220.txt>).

* * *

I'd like to talk to you about [a] widespread, but too little-challenged custom: earnings management. This process has evolved over the years into what can best be characterized as a game among market participants. A game that, if not addressed soon, will have adverse consequences for America's financial reporting system. A game that runs counter to the very principles behind our market's strength and success.

Increasingly, I have become concerned that the motivation to meet Wall Street earnings expectations may be overriding common sense business practices. Too many corporate managers, auditors, and analysts are participants in a game of nods and winks. In the zeal to satisfy consensus earnings estimates and project a smooth earnings path, wishful thinking may be winning the day over faithful representation.

As a result, I fear that we are witnessing an erosion in the quality of earnings, and therefore, the quality of financial reporting. Managing may be giving way to manipulation; integrity may be losing out to illusion.

Many in corporate America are just as frustrated and concerned about this trend as we, at the SEC, are. They know how difficult it is to hold the line on good practices when their competitors operate in the gray area between legitimacy and outright fraud.

A gray area where the accounting is being perverted; where managers are cutting corners; and, where earnings reports reflect the desires of management rather than the underlying financial performance of the company.

[I] want to talk about why integrity in financial reporting is under stress and explore five of the more common accounting gimmicks we've been seeing. Finally, I will outline a framework for a financial community response to this situation.

This necessary response involves improving both our accounting and disclosure rules, as well as the oversight and function of outside auditors and board audit committees. I am also calling upon a broad spectrum of capital market participants, from corporate management to Wall Street analysts to investors, to stand together and re-energize the touchstone of our financial reporting system: transparency and comparability.

This is a financial community problem. It can't be solved by a government mandate: it demands a financial community response.

THE ROLE OF FINANCIAL REPORTING IN OUR ECONOMY

Today, America's capital markets are the envy of the world. Our efficiency, liquidity and resiliency stand second to none. Our position, no doubt, has benefited from the opportunity and potential of the global economy. At the same time, however, this increasing interconnectedness has made us more susceptible to economic and financial weakness half a world away.

The significance of transparent, timely and reliable financial statements and its importance to investor protection has never been more apparent. The current financial situations in Asia and Russia are stark examples of this new reality. These markets are learning a painful lesson taught many times before: investors panic as a result of unexpected or unquantifiable bad news.

If a company fails to provide meaningful disclosure to investors about where it has been, where it is and where it is going, a damaging pattern ensues. The bond between shareholders and the company is shaken; investors grow anxious; prices fluctuate for no discernible reasons; and the trust that is the bedrock of our capital markets is severely tested.

THE PRESSURE TO "MAKE YOUR NUMBERS"

While the problem of earnings management is not new, it has swelled in a market that is unforgiving of companies that miss their estimates. I recently read of one major U.S. company, that failed to meet its so-called "numbers" by one penny, and lost more than six percent of its stock value in one day.

I believe that almost everyone in the financial community shares responsibility for fostering a climate in which earnings management is on the rise and the quality of financial reporting is on the decline. Corporate management isn't operating in a vacuum. In fact, the different pressures and expectations placed by, and on, various participants in the financial community appear to be almost self-perpetuating.

This is the pattern earnings management creates: companies try to meet or beat Wall Street earnings projections in order to grow market capitalization and increase the value of stock options. Their ability to do this depends on achieving the earnings expectations of analysts. And analysts seek constant guidance from companies to frame those expectations. Auditors, who want to retain their clients, are under pressure not to stand in the way.

ACCOUNTING HOCUS-POCUS

Our accounting principles weren't meant to be a straitjacket. Accountants are wise enough to know they cannot anticipate every business structure, or every new and innovative transaction, so they develop principles that allow for flexibility to adapt to changing circumstances. That's why the highest standards of objectivity, integrity and judgment can't be the exception. They must be the rule.

Flexibility in accounting allows it to keep pace with business innovations. Abuses such as earnings management occur when people exploit this pliancy. Trickery is employed to obscure actual financial volatility. This, in turn, masks the true consequences of management's decisions. These practices aren't limited to smaller companies struggling to gain investor interest. It's also happening in companies whose products we know and admire.

So what are these illusions? Five of the more popular ones I want to discuss today are "big bath" restructuring charges, creative acquisition accounting, "cookie jar reserves," "immaterial" misapplications of accounting principles, and the premature recognition of revenue.

"Big Bath" Charges

Let me first deal with "Big Bath" restructuring charges.

Companies remain competitive by regularly assessing the efficiency and profitability of their operations. Problems arise, however, when we see large charges associated with companies restructuring. These charges help companies "clean up" their balance sheet--giving them a so-called "big bath."

Why are companies tempted to overstate these charges? When earnings take a major hit, the theory goes, Wall Street will look beyond a one-time loss and focus only on future earnings.

And if these charges are conservatively estimated with a little extra cushioning, that so-called conservative estimate is miraculously reborn as income when estimates change or future earnings fall short.

When a company decides to restructure, management and employees, investors and creditors, customers and suppliers all want to understand the expected effects. We need, of course, to ensure that financial reporting provides this information. But this should not lead to flushing all the associated costs--and maybe a little extra--through the financial statements.

Creative Acquisition Accounting

Let me turn now to the second gimmick.

In recent years, whole industries have been remade through consolidations, acquisitions and spin-offs. Some acquirers, particularly those using stock as an acquisition currency, have used this environment as an opportunity to engage in another form of "creative" accounting. I call it "merger magic."

* * *

So what do [these acquirers] do? They classify an ever-growing portion of the acquisition price as "in-process" Research and Development, so--you guessed it--the amount can be written off in a "one-time" charge--removing any future earnings drag. Equally troubling is the creation of large liabilities for future operating expenses to protect future earnings--all under the mask of an acquisition.

Miscellaneous "Cookie Jar Reserves"

A third illusion played by some companies is using unrealistic assumptions to estimate liabilities for such items as sales returns, loan losses or warranty costs. In doing so, they stash accruals in cookie jars during the good times and reach into them when needed in the bad times.

I'm reminded of one U.S. company who took a large one-time loss to earnings to reimburse franchisees for equipment. That equipment, however, which included literally the kitchen sink, had yet to be bought. And, at the same time, they announced that future earnings would grow an impressive 15 percent per year.

"Materiality"

Let me turn now to the fourth gimmick--the abuse of materiality--a word that captures the attention of both attorneys and accountants. Materiality is another way we build flexibility into financial reporting. Using the logic of diminishing returns, some items may be so insignificant that they are not worth measuring and reporting with exact precision.

But some companies misuse the concept of materiality. They intentionally record errors within a defined percentage ceiling. They then try to excuse that fib by arguing that the effect on the bottom line is too small to matter. If that's the case, why do they work so hard to create these errors? Maybe because the effect can matter, especially if it picks up that last penny of the consensus estimate. When either management or the outside auditors are questioned about these clear violations of GAAP, they answer sheepishly[:] "It doesn't matter. It's immaterial."

In markets where missing an earnings projection by a penny can result in a loss of millions of dollars in market capitalization, I have a hard time accepting that some of these so-called non-events simply don't matter.

Revenue Recognition

Lastly, companies try to boost earnings by manipulating the recognition of revenue. Think about a bottle of fine wine. You wouldn't pop the cork on that bottle before it was ready. But some companies are doing this with their revenue--recognizing it before a sale is complete, before the product is delivered to a customer, or at a time when the customer still has options to terminate, void or delay the sale.

ACTION PLAN

Since U.S. capital market supremacy is based on the reliability and transparency of financial statements, this is a financial community problem that calls for timely financial community action.

Therefore, I am calling for immediate and coordinated action: technical rule changes by the regulators and standard setters to improve the transparency of financial statements; enhanced oversight of the financial reporting process by those entrusted as the shareholders' guardians; and nothing less than a fundamental cultural change on the part of corporate management as well as the whole financial community.

This action plan represents a cooperative public-private sector effort. It is essential that we work together to assure credibility and transparency. Our nine-point program calls for both regulators and the regulated to not only maintain, but increase public confidence which has made our markets the envy of the world. I believe this problem calls for immediate action that includes the following specific steps:

Improving the Accounting Framework

First, I have instructed the SEC staff to require well-detailed disclosures about the impact of changes in accounting assumptions. This should include a supplement to the financial statement showing beginning and ending balances as well as activity in between, including any adjustments. This will, I believe, enable the market to better understand the nature and effects of the restructuring liabilities and other loss accruals.

Second, we are challenging the profession, through the AICPA, to clarify the ground rules for auditing of purchased R&D. We also are requesting that they augment existing guidance on restructurings, large acquisition write-offs, and revenue recognition practices. It's time for the accounting profession to better qualify for auditors what's acceptable and what's not.

Third, I reject the notion that the concept of materiality can be used to excuse deliberate misstatements of performance. I know of one Fortune 500 company who had recorded a significant accounting error, and whose auditors told them so. But they still used a materiality ceiling of six percent earnings to justify the error. I have asked the SEC staff to focus on this problem and publish guidance that emphasizes the need to consider qualitative, not just quantitative factors of earnings. Materiality is not a bright line cutoff of three or five percent. It requires consideration of all relevant factors that could impact an investor's decision.

Fourth, SEC staff will immediately consider interpretive accounting guidance on the do's and don'ts of revenue recognition. The staff will also determine whether recently published standards for the software industry can be applied to other service companies.

Fifth, I am asking private sector standard setters to take action where current standards and guidance are inadequate. I encourage a prompt resolution of the FASB's projects, currently underway, that should bring greater clarity to the definition of a liability.

Sixth, the SEC's review and enforcement teams will reinforce these regulatory initiatives. We will formally target reviews of public companies that announce restructuring liability reserves, major write-offs or other practices that appear to manage earnings. Likewise, our enforcement team will continue to root out and aggressively act on abuses of the financial reporting process.

Improved Outside Auditing in the Financial Reporting Process

Seventh, I don't think it should surprise anyone here that recent headlines of accounting failures have led some people to question the thoroughness of audits. I need not remind auditors they are the public's watchdog in the financial reporting process. We rely on auditors to put something like the good housekeeping seal of approval on the information investors receive. The integrity of that information must take priority over a desire for cost efficiencies or competitive advantage in the audit process. High quality auditing requires well-trained, well-focused and well-supervised auditors.

As I look at some of the failures today, I can't help but wonder if the staff in the trenches of the profession have the training and supervision they need to ensure that audits are being done right. We cannot permit thorough audits to be sacrificed for re-engineered approaches that are efficient, but less effective. I have just proposed that the Public Oversight Board form a group of all the major constituencies to review the way audits are performed and assess the impact of recent trends on the public interest.

Strengthening the Audit Committee Process

And, finally, qualified, committed, independent and tough-minded audit committees represent the most reliable guardians of the public interest. Sadly, stories abound of audit committees whose members lack expertise in the basic principles of financial reporting as well as the mandate to ask probing questions. In fact, I've heard of one audit committee that convenes only twice a year before the regular board meeting for 15 minutes and whose duties are limited to a perfunctory presentation.

Compare that situation with the audit committee which meets twelve times a year before each board meeting; where every member has a financial background; where there are no personal ties to the chairman or the company; where they have their own advisers; where they ask tough questions of management and outside auditors; and where, ultimately, the investor interest is being served.

The SEC stands ready to take appropriate action if that interest is not protected. But, a private sector response that empowers audit committees and obviates the need for public sector dictates seems the wisest choice. I am pleased to announce that the financial community has agreed to accept this challenge.

As part eight of this comprehensive effort to address earnings management, the New York Stock Exchange and the National Association of Securities Dealers have agreed to sponsor a "blue-ribbon" panel to be headed by John Whitehead, former Deputy Secretary of State and retired senior partner of Goldman, Sachs, and Ira Millstein, a lawyer and noted corporate governance expert. Within the next 90 days, this distinguished group will develop a series of far-ranging recommendations intended to empower audit committees [to] function as the ultimate guardian of investor interests and corporate accountability. They are going to examine how we can get the right people to do the right things and ask the right questions.

Need for a Cultural Change

Finally, I'm challenging corporate management and Wall Street to re-examine our current environment. I believe we need to embrace nothing less than a cultural change. For corporate managers, remember, the integrity of the numbers in the financial reporting system is directly related to the long-term interests of a corporation. While the temptations are great, and the
pressures strong, illusions in numbers are only that--ephemeral, and ultimately self-destructive.

To Wall Street, I say, look beyond the latest quarter. Punish those who rely on deception, rather than the practice of openness and transparency.

CONCLUSION

Some may conclude that this debate is nothing more than an argument over numbers and legalistic terms. I couldn't disagree more.

* * *

Our mandate and our obligations are clear. We must rededicate ourselves to a fundamental principle: markets exist through the grace of investors.

Today, American markets enjoy the confidence of the world. How many half-truths, and how much accounting sleight-of-hand, will it take to tarnish that faith?

As a former businessman, I experienced all kinds of markets, dealt with a variety of trends, fads, fears, and irrational exuberances. I learned that some habits die hard. But, more than anything else, I learned that progress doesn't happen overnight and it's not sustained through short cuts or obfuscation. It's induced, rather, by asking hard questions and accepting difficult answers.

For the sake of our markets; for the sake of a globalized economy which depends so much on the reliability of America's financial system; for the sake of investors; and for the sake of a larger commitment not only to each other, but to ourselves, I ask that we join together to reinforce the values that have guided our capital markets to unparalleled supremacy. Together, through vigilance and trust, I know, we can succeed.

NOTES

1. Chapter IX in the casebook and the materials for that chapter in this supplement discuss "big bath" charges and creative acquisition accounting in more detail. See pages 703-710 of the casebook and *infra* at 99-100, 104-05. We will continue to discuss "cookie jar reserves" and revenue recognition in the supplemental materials for this chapter. Chapter II previously mentioned the "abuse of materiality." See *supra* at 33-34.

2. In a recent survey at a *Business Week* conference of chief financial officers, twelve percent admitted that "they had 'misrepresented corporate financial results' at the request of senior company executives," while fifty-five percent responded that "they had been asked to do so but 'fought off' the demand." Thor Valdmanis, *Accounting abracadabra[:] Cooking the books proves common trick of the trade*, USA Today, Aug. 11, 1998, at 1B; *see also* Eileen J. Williams, *Microcap, Financial Fraud, Reporting Violations At Top of List of Enforcement Priorities, SEC Staff Says*, Corp. Counsel Weekly, Mar. 24, 1999, at 5.

3. Accountants sometimes classify actions to manage earnings into two types: those which involve changing accounting methods and those which involve operating decisions. Adjusting the reserve, or the amount the enterprise has accrued as an expense to satisfy a contingency, illustrates a change in accounting method. In contrast, offering special terms to customers at year-end in an attempt to accelerate sales which would normally not occur until the next accounting period into the current accounting period exemplifies an operating decision. Marilyn Fischer & Kenneth Rosenzweig, *Attitudes of students and accounting practitioners concerning the ethical acceptability of earnings management*, 14 J. Bus. Ethics 433 (1995); see also Jennifer G. Hill, *Deconstructing Sunbeam–Contemporary Issues in Corporate Governance*, 67 U. Cin. L. Rev. 1099, 1103, 1127 (1999) (attributing the recent financial fraud at Sunbeam at least in part to "channel stuffing," a technique that artificially overstates earnings in one quarter at the expense of later quarters, and concluding that a commercial culture that stress short-term profit maximization, combined with remuneration orthodoxy that attempts to align managerial and shareholder interests, provides strong incentives for manipulating accounting records). Should the distinction between the two types of earnings management matter?

4. You may recall from the discussion in Chapter II of the casebook on page 148 that given the various permissible choices in alternative accounting treatments, some companies could select from more than a million possible bottom lines. If no true "bottom line" exists, do earnings management and income smoothing simply reflect efforts by businesses "'to put their best foot forward?'" *See, e.g.*, Thor Valdmanis, *Accounting abracadabra[:] Cooking the books proves common trick of the trade*, USA Today, Aug. 11, 1998, at 1B (quoting Robert Olstein); *see also* Claire A. Hill, *Why Financial Appearances Might Matter: An Explanation for "Dirty Pooling" and Some Other Types of Financial Cosmetics*, 22 Del. J. Corp. L. 141(1997) (discussing various "beautification techniques" that enterprises use to increase or smooth reported earnings and offering an explanation for their existence).

5. As its most visible actions during the period beginning shortly before Chairman Levitt's speech on "The 'Numbers Game'" and continuing to the present, the SEC has brought well-publicized enforcement actions against at least three registrants and high-ranking officers at those companies for managing earnings and promised to continue its crusade.

About three months before the speech, the SEC instituted public administrative proceedings against Venator Group, Inc., the company formerly known as Woolworth Corporation ("Woolworth"), and four former senior officers in response to a scheme to manage Woolworth's reported earnings. In the cease-and-desist proceeding against Woolworth, which the company settled by agreeing to cease and desist from future financial reporting violations without admitting or denying the Commission's allegations, the SEC found that the former officers at Woolworth and two of its major subsidiaries, Kinney Shoe Corporation ("Kinney") and Woolworth Canada Inc. ("Canada"), engaged in a scheme to manage the company's reported earnings by inflating profits by understating cost of sales and improperly deferring certain operating expenses that the subsidiaries incurred in the first two quarters of the company's 1993 fiscal year. This fraudulent conduct enabled Woolworth to report a profit for each of the first two quarters of fiscal 1993, even though the company actually lost money during those quarters. The former officers then adjusted results in the third and fourth quarters, so that the company could report accurate results by year-end, when the outside auditor examined the company's financial statements. In re Venator Group, Inc., Accounting and Auditing Enforcement Release No. 1049, [1995-1998 Transfer Binder] Fed. Sec. L. Rep. (CCH) ¶ 74,564 (1998).

Less than three months after Chairman Levitt's speech, the SEC announced a civil action against W.R. Grace & Co. ("Grace") and public administrative and cease-and-desist proceedings against seven former executives, including the company's former president and chief financial officer, for financial fraud involving earnings manipulation. The complaint in the civil action alleges that Grace, through its subsidiary National Medical Care, Inc., falsely reported operating results between 1991 and 1995 by deferring income to smooth earnings. Rather than report the income, the Company allegedly established reserves that did not conform with GAAP and then used those reserves to manipulate quarterly and annual earnings. The SEC's complaint further alleges that when Grace reversed the excess reserves during the 1995 fourth quarter, the company improperly netted the excess reserves with other amounts and "misleadingly described the reversal as a 'change in accounting estimate.'" SEC v. W.R. Grace & Co., Accounting and Auditing Enforcement Release No. 1091, [1995-1998 Transfer Binder] Fed. Sec. L. Rep. (CCH) ¶ 74,599F (1998); In re Bolduc, Accounting and Auditing Enforcement Release No. 1090, [1995-1998 Transfer Binder] Fed. Sec. L. Rep. (CCH) ¶ 74,599E (1998). In 1999, Grace consented to a cease-and-desist order and agreed to set aside $1 million to establish a fund, and then to use that fund within one year, to develop at least one program to further awareness and education relating to financial statements and generally accepted accounting principles. In re W.R. Grace & Co., Accounting and Auditing Enforcement Release No. 1140, 7 Fed. Sec. L. Rep. (CCH) ¶ 74,647 (1999).

In 1999, the SEC instituted public administrative proceedings against Terex Corporation, its former chairman, and an affiliate for overstating Terex's pre-tax earnings by at least $77.3 million in its 1989 through 1991 annual and quarterly reports. Without admitting or denying the misconduct, the respondents agreed to cease and desist from future financial reporting violations. Terex's financial statements overstated the company's income by improperly excluding losses from certain subsidiaries and using undisclosed reserves that the company had previously established. In addition, Terex's Management's Discussion and Analysis sections during that period did not reveal that the undisclosed, nonrecurring adjustments from the reserves had enhanced the company's operating results and financial condition. Perhaps most significantly, the agreed Order specifically states that "Item 303(a) [of Regulation S-K, Management's Discussion and Analysis of Financial Condition and Results of Operations,] requires that management address any issues which impact the quality of earnings." In re Terex Corp., Accounting and Auditing Enforcement Release No. 1126, 7 Fed. Sec. L. Rep. (CCH) ¶ 74,633 (1999).

In late 1999, SEC Enforcement Director Richard Walker told attendees at the AICPA's annual National Conference on Current SEC Developments that the SEC plans to criminally prosecute those individuals that manage earnings. He stated: "'We are turning the numbers game into a Monopoly game. That is, cook the books and you will go directly to jail.'" Ronald Taylor, *Hunt Warns Accountants Against Continuing to 'Push the Envelope,'* 31 Sec. Reg. & L. Rep. (BNA) 1636 (1999).

6. The SEC continues to oversee the financial community's efforts to improve financial accounting and reporting and to work on initiatives related to the agency's agenda to curb "earnings management." The SEC has issued proposed rules to specify the disclosures that registrants must provide concerning changes in valuation and loss accrual accounts. Supplementary Financial Information, 65 Fed. Reg. 4585 (2000) (proposed Jan. 31, 2000). The SEC staff has also published staff accounting bulletins on materiality, restructuring charges, and revenue recognition. Materiality, Staff Accounting Bulletin No. 99, 64 Fed. Reg. 45,150 (1999), reprinted in 7 Fed. Sec. L. Rep. (CCH) ¶ 75,501, at 64,219-3 (Dec. 8, 1999); Restructuring and Impairment Charges, Staff Accounting Bulletin No. 100, 64 Fed. Reg. 67,154 (1999), reprinted in 7 Fed. Sec. L. Rep. (CCH) ¶¶ 75,705, 75,721 at 64,227-3, 64,228, 64,269-70, 64,291-96 (Dec. 8, 1999); Revenue Recognition in Financial Statements, Staff Accounting Bulletin No. 101, 64 Fed. Reg. 1,122,290 (1999), reprinted in 7 Fed. Sec. Reg. L. Rep. (CCH) ¶ ¶ 75,735, 75,761, at 64,341-42 (Jan. 12, 2000), 64,421-34 (Dec. 15, 1999 & Apr. 12, 2000); Revenue Recognition in Financial Statements, Staff Accounting Bulletin No. 101A, Amendment: Revenue Recognition in Financial Statements, 65 Fed. Reg. 16,811 (2000), reprinted in 7 Fed. Sec. Reg. L. Rep. (CCH) ¶ 75,761 at 64,432-34 (Dec. 15, 1999 & Apr. 12, 2000). In addition to the enforcement actions described in the previous note, the SEC has also notified more than 150 publicly traded companies that the staff may review their 1998 annual reports for various issues, including asset write-downs, restructuring activities, charges related to acquired research and development, and provisions for bad loans and other uncollectible accounts. Steve Burkholder, *SEC Notifies 150-Plus Companies Of Possible Review of Write-Downs Reporting*, 31 Sec. Reg. & L. Rep. (BNA) 153 (1999).

In January 1999, the AICPA issued new guidance on revenue recognition and earlier established a special working group on in-process research and development to publish a "best practices" document. Meanwhile, the FASB's agenda includes rulemaking projects on those obligations that require an enterprise to recognize a liability, especially obligations arising from the retirement of long-lived assets, and impairment and asset disposal issues. As already mentioned, *supra* at 14-15, the Blue Ribbon Committee on Improving the Effectiveness of Corporate Audit Committees has submitted its report and offered its recommendations. The SEC has issued final rules that implement many of those recommendations. See *supra* at 15. Finally, the Public Oversight Board's special panel on audit effectiveness has issued a draft report. See *supra* at 30. Steve Burkholder, *AICPA Issues Guidance Amid SEC Concerns About Practice*, 31 Sec. Reg. & L. Rep. (BNA) 155 (1999); Steve Burkholder, *SEC Warns 'In-Process R&D' Writeoffs In Mergers Could Lead to Restatements*, 30 Sec. Reg. & L. Rep. (BNA) 1454 (1998).

1. An Exchange Transaction

a. NATURE OF THE EXCHANGE TRANSACTION

(1) In General

b) SHAMS

Page 381. Insert the following at the end of note 1:

More recently, the SEC dismissed a disciplinary action that arose from the transactions in the "second and third quarter programs" and that the Division of Enforcement brought against Warren G. Trepp, the former head trader in the high yield bond department of the now defunct Drexel Burnham Lambert Inc. ("Drexel"). The SEC's order stated that issuing a cease-and-desist order would not serve any remedial purpose under the circumstances. In re Trepp, 70 S.E.C. Docket 1526 (1999), 1999 WL 753922 (S.E.C.). About two years earlier, an administrative law judge ("ALJ") found that Reliance and Drexel carried out an illegal "parking agreement," which means that in a purported sale of securities, the "seller" secretly agrees to repurchase the securities from the "buyer" at a later date, typically in an attempt to obtain false tax losses or to avoid legal requirements under the federal securities laws. The ALJ also found that Trepp caused Drexel to violate the federal securities laws because he did not disclose the underlying "parking agreement" on the firm's trading tickets. Although the ALJ found that Reliance also violated various securities laws, she concluded that Trepp did not cause Reliance's violations because of his remoteness in the chain of causation. Because Trepp's violations occurred nine years before the SEC instituted the proceeding, the Commission did not introduce any evidence to suggest recurrent violations in the interim, and Trepp had not worked in the securities industry since 1992, the ALJ concluded that no reasonable likelihood of future violations existed and declined to issue a cease and desist order against him. In re Trepp, 65 S.E.C. Docket 512, 1997 WL 469718 (S.E.C.).

Page 381. Insert the following note after note 2:

2A. The principal case illustrates "cherry picking," a technique that some enterprises used to "smooth" or "manage" earnings before FASB adopted FASB Statement No. 130, *supra* at 45-46, on reporting comprehensive income. When an enterprise held securities that had appreciated in value over the enterprise's original cost, the enterprise could recognize gain at any time by selling some or all of the securities and reporting the resulting gain on the income statement. Such gains could mask losses from operating activities. Please note that without the "cherry picking" Reliance would have reported a $22.5 million net loss in the second quarter of 1986, a $6.0 million net loss in the third quarter, and $23.9 million in net income for the entire fiscal year, rather than the net incomes actually reported for those periods of $7.8 million, $2.8 million and $63 million, respectively. This illustration also demonstrates the need to consider nonrecurring items carefully in evaluating the operating results for a particular accounting period.

Page 390. After the principal case, insert the following as note 1 and renumber existing note 1 as note 1A:

1. The legal saga arising from the criminal actions against Charles Keating, Jr. and his son, Charles Keating III, has finally ended. In early 1998, the United States Court of Appeals for the Ninth Circuit reinstated the father's California securities fraud convictions, concluding that the District Court relied on a repudiated decision when it granted federal habeas corpus relief in 1996. The Ninth Circuit ordered the petition for habeas corpus "dismissed without prejudice." Keating v. Hood, 133 F.3d 1240 (9th Cir. 1998). In April 1999, Charles Keating, Jr. pled guilty to three counts of wire fraud and one count of bankruptcy fraud for transferring $975,000 out of ACC as "loans" to himself, his son and his son-in-law, two weeks before ACC declared bankruptcy. Following his guilty plea, the District Court sentenced Keating to the fifty months that he had already served in federal prison. Although a federal jury had previously convicted both Keatings on federal racketeering, conspiracy, bank fraud, securities fraud and mail fraud charges in 1993, the District Court subsequently ordered a new trial on the grounds that some jurors had learned about and discussed the Keatings' state court convictions. The Ninth Circuit later affirmed the District Court's decision. United States v. Keating, 147 F.3d 895 (9th Cir. 1998). At the time of the father's guilty plea, "[t]he government also announced that it dismissed the case against Keating's son, Charles Keating III, because of the passage of time and 'in the interest of justice.'" Tom Gilroy, *Charles Keating Jr. Pleads Guilty To Federal Fraud in Thrift Case*, 31 Sec. Reg. & L. Rep. (BNA) 500 (1999).

Page 391. Following note 3 at the top of the page, insert the following new note:

4. The conveyance of a financial asset other than cash by and to someone other than the financial asset's issuer in circumstances where the transferor has some continuing involvement either with the asset transferred or with the transferee often presents difficult accounting questions about "substance" and whether the parties should treat the transfer as a sale of all or part of the asset or as a secured borrowing. These circumstances can include transfers of partial interests; repurchase agreements; transfers of receivables with recourse, which means that the transferee can receive repayment from the transferor if the debtors fail to pay when due; securitizations, or the process by which an issuer assembles pools of various financial assets, such as mortgage loan or credit card receivables, and sells partial interests in those pools as securities which entitle the purchaser to a prorata share of both the interest and return of principal as the borrowers repay the underlying obligations; arrangements where the transferor agrees to service a mortgage loan or credit card receivable; and situations where the transferor owns an equity interest in the transferee. In FASB Statement No. 125, *Accounting for Transfers and Servicing of Financial Assets and Extinguishments of Liabilities*, the FASB recently adopted an approach that focuses on control in determining a transaction's "substance." If the transferor surrenders economic control over an asset, the parties account for the transfer as a sale to the extent that the transferor receives consideration other than a beneficial interest in the transferred asset. Accounting for Transfers and Servicing of Financial Assets and Extinguishments of Liabilities, Statement of Financial Accounting Standards No. 125 (Financial Accounting Standards Bd. 1996). In that event, the transferor removes the asset from its balance sheet. As a practical matter, banks often want sales treatment to satisfy regulatory requirements that they maintain certain minimum capital reserves. If the transferor does not surrender economic control, FASB Statement No. 125 treats the transaction as a secured borrowing and the asset remains on the transferor's balance sheet. *See* Steve Burkholder, *FASB Considers FDIC Powers as Receiver, Effect on Financial Asset Transfer Accounting*, 30 Sec. Reg. & L. Rep. (BNA) 772 (1998).

As one of several conditions necessary to surrender economic control, a conveyance must separate or "isolate" the relevant asset from the transferor, meaning that the transfer must "put [the asset] presumptively beyond the reach of the transferor and its creditors, even in bankruptcy or other receivership." Accounting for Transfers and Servicing of Financial Assets and Extinguishments of Liabilities, Statement of Financial Accounting Standard No. 125, ¶ 9a (Financial Accounting Standards Bd. 1996). In this regard, Appendix A to FASB Statement No. 125 further provides generally that a transferor can remove conveyed assets from its balance sheet only if the "available evidence provides reasonable assurance" that a bankruptcy trustee or other receiver for the transferor or any of its affiliates could not legally reach the transferred assets. *Id.*, ¶ 23. Because this standard involves legal questions, a recent interpretation of SAS No. 73, Using the Work of a Specialist, specifically allows auditors to use legal opinions as evidential matter to support management's assertion that a transfer of a financial asset satisfies the isolation criterion in FASB Statement No. 125 and offers guidelines for using such opinions for transactions entered into on or after January 1, 1998. The Use of Legal Interpretations As Evidential Matter to Support Management's Assertion That a Transfer of Financial Assets Has Met the Isolation Criterion in Paragraph 9(a) of Financial Accounting Standards Board Statement No. 125, Auditing Interpretation No. 1 of Statement of Auditing Standards No. 73 (American Inst. of Certified Pub.

Accountants 1998), *reprinted in* American Institute of Certified Public Accountants, 1 Professional Standards at AU § 9336 (Jan. 1998).

After the interpretation's release, the Committee on Legal Opinions of the American Bar Association's Section of Business Law expressed concerns that allowing the client's auditor to review the opinion might create privity between the lawyer and the auditor. In an attempt to avoid this risk and in consultation with the ASB, the Committee on Legal Opinions and the Committee of Law and Accounting drafted a form letter to accompany all "true sale" opinions that lawyers might issue to clients and make available to auditors. Effective October 1, 1998, the ASB amended the interpretation to reflect acceptance of the form letter. *Is it a true sale?*, Bus. L. Today, March/April 1999, at 64.

As a result of these recent pronouncements, bankruptcy and commercial lawyers can expect to encounter requests for such opinions in their practices and should develop an understanding of the underlying accounting principles and auditing standards.   In particular, lawyers representing federally regulated financial institutions should exercise extreme caution in rendering opinions. The Financial Institutions Reform and Recovery Act of 1989 gives the Federal Deposit Insurance Corporation ("FDIC") broad statutory powers to repudiate some contracts and to reclaim transferred assets, by paying principal and interest to the date of receivership. Although rarely invoked except in cases of fraud or other improper conduct, the powers prevented knowledgcable attorneys from rendering so-called "true sale at law opinions" on transfers by financial institutions. As a result, the FASB originally planned to amend FASB Statement No. 125 to state explicitly that the FDIC's broad powers preclude sales accounting. After the FDIC staff published a proposed statement that stated that, subject to certain conditions, the FDIC would not attempt to reclaim or recover such transferred assets, however, FASB concluded that FASB Statement No. 125 no longer needed such specific guidance about the effect of the FDIC's powers as receiver. Accounting for Transfers of Financial Assets–an amendment of FASB Statement No. 125, Proposed Statement of Financial Accounting Standards ¶¶13-16 (Financial Accounting Standards Bd. 1999). In the meantime, the EITF concluded that FDIC's presumed broader powers to reclaim transferred assets do not preclude sale accounting for transfers under paragraph 9(a) of FASB Statement No. 125. Steve Burkholder, *FASB Issues Update on Financial Assets Transfers, FDIC Powers*, 30 Sec. Reg. & L. Rep. (BNA) 1330 (1998); Steve Burkholder, *FASB Considers FDIC Powers as Receiver, Effect on Financial Asset Transfer Accounting*, 30 Sec. Reg. & L. Rep. (BNA) 772, 773 (1998) (also reporting that the FASB has tentatively decided to reaffirm its position that a transfer qualifies as "close enough" to isolation even though a bankruptcy trustee or other receiver could later reclaim the transferred asset by paying principal and interest to the date of payment).

Many issues in this very complex area, however, remain unsettled. In June 1999, the FASB issued an exposure draft to amend FASB Statement No. 125. Accounting for Transfers of Financial Assets–an amendment of FASB Statement No. 125, Proposed Statement of Financial Accounting Standards (Financial Accounting Standards Bd. 1999). In addition, the FASB staff has already released three questions and answers publications and a proposed Technical Bulletin, whose final issuance the staff subsequently decided to postpone until the staff and Board can consider the relationship between the technical bulletin and the proposed amendment to FASB Statement No. 125. The FASB currently plans to issue a final amendment to FASB Statement No. 125 in the third quarter of 2000.

(2) Special Circumstances

a) NONMONETARY EXCHANGES

Page 402. After note 2, insert the following note:

3. Plaintiffs-appellants brought the principal case as a federal securities fraud claim. Exclusive jurisdiction for such actions lies in the federal courts. After the Private Securities Litigation Reform Act of 1995 added statutory safe harbors for forward-looking statements to the federal securities laws, skillful litigants began bringing state securities fraud actions in state courts to avoid the federal safe harbors. In the Securities Litigation Uniform Standards Act of 1998, Congress tried to close this loophole by requiring plaintiffs to bring most lawsuits involving nationally traded securities in federal court under uniform federal standards. This most recent legislation, however, does not apply to lawsuits based upon the law of the enterprise's state of incorporation or organization and regarding certain communications to holders of the enterprise's equity interests, the so-called "Delaware carve-out." In *Malone v. Brincat*, 722 A.2d 5 (Del. 1998), the Supreme Court of Delaware recognized a potential cause of action for breach of fiduciary duty under Delaware law, even in the absence of a request for shareholder action, based upon the defendant directors' failure to disclose accurate information about Mercury Finance Company's earnings, financial performance and shareholders' equity. As a result, financial frauds may increasingly give rise to state claims alleging breach of the fiduciary duty to disclose accurate information. *See, e.g.*, Lalondriz v. USA Networks, Inc., 68 F. Supp. 2d 285 (S.D.N.Y. 1999) (denying a motion for reconsideration of an earlier order remanding a class action that alleged breach of fiduciary duty under Delaware law to the state court in New York where plaintiff filed the original complaint, but commenting that the earlier order did not intend to describe the cause of action as inside or outside the "Delaware carve-out").

b) RELATED PARTY TRANSACTIONS

Page 403. Before the carryover sentence at the bottom of the page, insert the following:

The SEC has recently brought several enforcement actions against enterprises and officers that failed to disclose related party transactions or that presented false and misleading information regarding such transactions. *See, e.g.*, In re Audre Recognition Systems, Inc., Accounting and Auditing Enforcement Release No. 1076, [1995-1998 Transfer Binder] Fed. Sec. L. Rep. (CCH) ¶ 74,590 (1998) (company's chairman, president and chief executive officer obtained a $908,000 personal loan from the company and directed various subordinates to withhold disclosure, create false records and misrepresent the transactions to the company's auditors and later to conceal the circumstances surrounding the earlier nondisclosure); In re DeGeorge Financial Corporation, Accounting and Auditing Enforcement Release No. 984, 7 Fed. Sec. L. Rep. (CCH) ¶ 74,499 (1997) (chief executive officer used at least $680,000 of the company's money to fund a triathlon team he operated and managed, to finance a private business venture marketing a fat loss product, and to pay his personal legal expenses and directed company employees to manage and operate his private company which owned a portfolio of mortgages, to monitor construction of his home, and to enter into other transactions which provided favorable terms to his relatives); In re Koinis, Accounting and Auditing Enforcement Release No. 917, 7 Fed. Sec. L. Rep. (CCH) ¶ 74,432 (1997)(company retained PRK Group, Inc. ("PRK"), a newly formed related party owned one-third each by the wife of the company's board chairman and chief executive officer, the wife of the company president and chief operating officer, and the company's outside securities counsel, and paid PRK $219,220 in fees and disbursements for alleged investment banking services that the related party did not in fact render).

b. EXCEPTIONS TO THE EXCHANGE TRANSACTION REQUIREMENT

Page 405. Before the first full sentence at the top of the page, insert the following:

Starting for fiscal periods beginning after December 15, 1997, enterprises must include changes in the balance of these unrealized holding gains and losses as a component of "comprehensive income." As discussed below, *infra* at 82-85, although enterprises need not use the term "comprehensive income," they must report the total change in net assets, or owners' equity, from all transactions, other events, and circumstances that did not involve owners during an accounting period, including any change in net unrealized holding gain and loss, somewhere in the financial statements.

2. EARNINGS PROCESS SUBSTANTIALLY COMPLETE

a. GENERAL RULES

Page 425. Near the bottom of the page, insert the following new sections:

(4) Software Revenue Recognition

As the computer software industry has grown in importance in this country, the accounting profession has recognized the need for specific revenue recognition rules for software transactions. These transactions can range from agreements that provide a license for a single software product to arrangements that require the supplying enterprise not only to deliver software or a software system, but also to expend significant efforts to produce, modify or customize the software. Concluding a five-year project, the AICPA recently released Statement of Position 97-2, *Software Revenue Recognition*, which generally tightens the revenue recognition rules in the area for transactions entered into during fiscal years beginning after December 15, 1997.

Although the following discussion does not attempt to describe the new rules in any detail, several general statements can convey the rules' importance. If a software transaction does not require significant production, modification or customization services, the vendor should recognize revenue when the transaction meets the following four criteria: (1) persuasive evidence of the arrangement, such as a signed contract, purchase order or on-line authorization, exists; (2) delivery has occurred; (3) the arrangement fixes the vendor's fee or allows its determination; *and* (4) collectibility appears probable. In contrast, when a transaction requires the supplying enterprise to perform significant production, modification or customization activities, the vendor must follow the rules for long-term contracts that the casebook discusses on pages 430 to 440. Those rules either limit the enterprise's ability to recognize revenue to an amount that represents the actual percentage of estimated work that the enterprise actually performed during the period or force the vendor to wait until substantially completing the required services before recognizing any revenue.

Collectively, the new rules require vendors to defer revenue on software contracts if the vendor has not yet provided all the promised services or software components. In the past, software enterprises enjoyed the leeway to record revenue upon delivery of the first part of the software package. As a result, the new rules may force enterprise to delay the recording of revenues for months, or even years. Software Revenue Recognition, Statement of Position 97-2 (Accounting Standards Division, American Inst. of Certified Pub. Accountants 1997); *see also* Deferral of the Effective Date of a Provision of SOP 97-2, *Software Revenue Recognition*, Statement of Position 98-4 (Accounting Standards Division, American Inst. of Certified Pub. Accountants 1998); Modification of SOP 97-2, Software Revenue Recognition, With Respect to Certain Transactions, Statement of Position 98-9 (Accounting Standards Division, American Inst. of Certified Pub. Accountants 1998); Melody Petersen, *Accounting Rule Hurts Software Companies' Revenues*, N.Y. Times, April 30, 1998, at D1.

(5) Revenue Recognition and the Internet

As the Internet and e-commerce exploded during the late 1990s, interesting and important accounting questions have emerged. With the business community and financial markets often using multiples of revenues to value Internet firms, the determination of revenues becomes crucial. The following six situations illustrate the revenue recognition issues that have arisen.

Situation One. A purchaser buys an item from an Internet auction company's customer for $1,000. Under the customer's agreement with the Internet auction company, the customer must remit ten percent of the sales price to the Internet firm.

Situation Two. An Internet auction company distributes goods for a wholesale supplier. The company incurs no obligation to pay the supplier until the purchaser actually pays for the goods. The Internet auction company sells goods for $1,000. When the purchaser remits the $1,000, the company electronically transfers $800 to the supplier's bank account.

Situation Three. An Internet service provider ("ISP") offers a $400 rebate to purchasers of personal computers who contract for three years of Internet service at $25 per month.

Situation Four. A purchaser buys an item from an Internet company for $25, plus $3 shipping and handling, uses a $15 coupon, and remits $13.

Situation Five. An Internet company offers "free" overnight shipping. A customer buys an item for $25. The company pays $10 to ship the item overnight.

Situation Six. Two Internet companies enter into a barter agreement agree in which they agree to "purchase" advertising space on each other's Internet site. The agreement sets the value of the advertising on each site at $100,000. One company charges other customers $90,000 for similar advertising services. The other company plans to unveil its Internet site within sixty days and has never sold advertising space to anyone else.

How should these Internet companies account for each of these transactions? How much should they report as revenues? What amounts, if any, should they record as cost of goods sold or marketing expenses? *See* Revenue Recognition in Financial Statements, Staff Accounting Bulletin No. 101, 64 Fed. Reg. 1,122,290 (1999), reprinted in 7 Fed. Sec. Reg. L. Rep. (CCH) ¶ 75,565 (Apr. 12, 2000); Accounting for Coupons, Rebates, and Discounts, Emerging Issues Task Force Issue No. 00-14 (Financial Accounting Standards Bd. 2000); Accounting for Shipping and Handling Revenues and Costs, Emerging Issues Task Force Issue No. 00-10 (Financial Accounting Standards Bd. tentative conclusion reached at May 17-18, 2000 meeting); Reporting Revenue Gross as a Principal versus Net as an Agent, Emerging Issues Task Force Issue No. 99-19 (Financial Accounting Standards Bd. last discussed at May 17-18, 2000 meeting of the Emerging Issues Task Force); Accounting for Advertising Barter Transactions, Emerging Issues Task Force Issue No. 99-17 (Financial Accounting Standards Bd. 2000); *see also* Matt Krantz, *CDnow gains in question[;] E-retailer counts coupons as sales*, USA Today, Dec. 6, 1999, at 1B; Elizabeth MacDonald, *Concerns on Internet Firms' Accounting Prompt SEC to Seek Tighter Standards*, Wall St. J., Nov. 18, 1999, at A4.

C. THE MATCHING PRINCIPLE FOR EXPENSES

2. ACCRUAL OF EXPENSES AND LOSSES

b. THE PROBLEM OF UNCOLLECTIBLE ACCOUNTS

Page 473. At the end of the carryover paragraph at the top of the page, insert the following discussion:

As an example of the "miscellaneous 'cookie jar reserves'" that SEC Chairman Arthur Levitt described as the "third [accounting] illusion," he specifically listed "loan losses." See *supra* at 66. These loan losses are nothing more than the "Bad Debt Expense" for the estimated uncollectible amounts in the loan portfolio of a bank or other financial institution. As one of the its financial reporting initiatives following Chairman Levitt's "The 'Numbers Game'" remarks, the SEC expressed concern that financial institutions have intentionally created and maintained large reserves, or allowances for loan losses, in good economic times to pad against potential losses during economic downturns. During its acquisition of Crestar Financial Corp., SunTrust Banks Inc. agreed with the SEC in November 1998 to revise its reported earnings and reduce its expenses for loan losses by $100 million for the three-year period from 1994 to 1996. Seeking to avoid another savings and loan-type crisis, banking regulators have repeatedly cautioned banks to manage credit risk exposure prudently and warned that the SEC's efforts could cause banks to ignore conservatism and to cut reserves for loan losses.

During 1998 and 1999, the SEC and federal bank regulators announced a series of joint agreements to work with the public accounting and banking industries to develop new guidance to ensure that loan loss reserves remain adequate, while guarding against inappropriate earnings manipulation. The first agreement affirms that financial institutions should strive to link loan loss reserves to specific bad loans, and "include a 'margin for imprecision' that reflects the uncertainty associated with estimating probable credit losses in their loan portfolios.'" A second agreement announced plans to work together to issue guidance for financial institutions on the appropriate assessment and disclosure of potential loan losses. After a controversial SEC announcement which instructed banks to follow guidance in an April 1999 *Viewpoints* article entitled "Application of FASB Statements 5 and 114 to a Loan Portfolio"in accounting for loan loss reserves, even if doing so meant making a one-time adjustment to loan loss allowances, reignited the controversy, the SEC announced its agreement to consult with banking regulators before determining whether to take any significant action on loan loss reserves reported in a bank's financial statements. During the controversy, the U.S. House of Representatives approved an amendment to its version of the financial services reform bill, which Congress ultimately included in the final legislation, to require the SEC to "consult and coordinate comments with the appropriate Federal banking agency before taking any action or rendering any opinion" on how any insured banking institution should report loan loss reserves in its financial statements. Gramm-Leach-Bliley Act, Pub. L. No. 106-102, § 241(a) (1999). More recently, the FASB gave the AICPA's

Accounting Standards Executive Committee permission to proceed with a project on loan loss allowances that could result in a final statement of position by mid-2001. Steve Burkholder, *AICPA to Move Forward With Project on Loan Loss Allowances*, 31 Sec. Reg. & L. Rep. (BNA) 1236 (1999); Ali Sartipzadeh, *SEC, Bank Regulators Have Consensus On Loan Loss Allowance Issue, Levitt Says*, 31 Sec. Reg. & L. Rep. (BNA) 1029 (1999); Eileen Canning, *Banking Agencies, SEC Clarify Guidance on Loan Loss Reserves, Ease Controversy*, 31 Sec. Reg. & L. Rep. (BNA) 952 (1999); Alex D. McElroy, *Bank, Securities Agencies Agree to Develop Consistent Guidance on Loan Loss Reserves*, 30 Sec. Reg. & L. Rep. (BNA) 1726 (1998); Alex D. McElroy, *Bank Agencies, SEC Clash on SunTrust Case, Pledge to Clarify Loan Loss Reserve Policies*, 30 Sec. Reg. & L. Rep. (BNA) 1676 (1998).

c. MATCHING EXPENSES FOR INCOME TAX PURPOSES

Page 478. Following note 2 at the top of the page, insert the following new note:

3.   A recent law review article argues that the matching principle serves no independent value in our federal income tax system and can actually conflict with true tax values that recognize the time value of money and the difference between an income tax and a consumption tax.   Deborah A. Geier, *The Myth of the Matching Principle as a Tax Value*, 15 Am. J. Tax Policy 17 (1998).

D. INCOME STATEMENT PRESENTATION AND DISCLOSURE

Page 484.   Before the "Prior Period Adjustments" heading, insert the following:

As discussed earlier, *supra* at 45-46, in 1997 the FASB issued FASB Statement No. 130, *Reporting Comprehensive Income*, which requires enterprises to report an amount for "comprehensive income" in the financial statements for fiscal years beginning after December 15, 1997.   The pronouncement defines "comprehensive income" as "the change in equity [net assets] of a business enterprise during a period from transactions and other events and circumstances from nonowner sources." Previously, enterprises reported most changes in equity from nonowner sources on the income statement; some nonowner changes in equity, however, such as the unrealized gains and losses from holding "available-for-sale" marketable securities, did not affect the income statement, and appeared only in a separate component of the equity section of the balance sheet.

FASB Statement No. 130 divides "comprehensive income" into "net income" and "other comprehensive income."   "Net income" includes income from continuing operations, discontinued operations, extraordinary items, and cumulative effects of changes in accounting principles.   "Other comprehensive income" includes foreign currency items, minimum pension liability adjustments, and the unrealized gain or loss on certain investments in debt and equity securities. The new pronouncement does not require a specific format to report "comprehensive income" but does mandate that an enterprise display an amount representing total nonowner changes in equity for the period somewhere in the financial statements. As a result, enterprises may use: (i) a "statement of income and comprehensive income," (ii) separate statements for "traditional" net income and comprehensive income, (iii) a "statement of changes in equity," or (iv) some other format to present the required information. Note that Ben & Jerry's 1999 consolidated financial statements, which you can find in the appendix to this supplement, use the third alternative, combined with additional disclosures in the notes to the financial statements. See *infra* at pages 134-35 and 141-42. If an enterprise does not have any items of "other comprehensive income" during an accounting period, the enterprise need not report a separate amount for "comprehensive income." Reporting Comprehensive Income, Statement of Financial Accounting Standards No. 130 (Financial Accounting Standards Bd. 1997).

To illustrate the concept of comprehensive income, assume that, as its only investment, Vogt Corporation ("Vogt"), a calender year corporation, purchases 10,000 shares of Keller, Inc. ("Keller"), a publicly traded corporation with total market value exceeding $1 billion, on March 1, Year 1 for $100,000 (i.e., $10 per share). Further assume that by the end of Year 1, the market value of each share of Keller stock has increased to $13 per share. At the end of Year 2, the market price equals $18 per share. On February 1, Year 3, Vogt sells its Keller shares for $17 per share. How much income and comprehensive income does Vogt recognize from these events?

At the time of the original investment, Vogt would make the following journal entry:

Investments (debit)	$100,000	
Cash (credit)		$100,000

As available-for-sale securities, the Keller shares will appear on Vogt's balance sheet at the end of Year 1 and 2 at their fair values of $130,000 and $180,000, respectively. The increase in value would appear in a separate section of shareholders' equity. At the end of Year 1, Vogt would make the following journal entry to reflect the increase in fair value:

Investments (debit)	$30,000	
Unrealized Gain on Marketable Equity		
Securities (credit) (an equity account)		$30,000

After the $30,000 debit to the Investments account, that account would show a $130,000 debit balance. In addition to appearing in the equity section of the balance sheet, the $30,000 unrealized gain would appear in both "other comprehensive income" and comprehensive income. Although Vogt would not recognize any net income from the increase in fair value (because no exchange transaction has occurred), the company's financial statements would show $30,000 in "other comprehensive income" and comprehensive income of $30,000 ($-0- net income plus $30,000 in "other comprehensive income").

At the end of Year 2, Vogt would make the following journal entry to reflect the increase in the fair value of the Keller shares to $180,000 during the year:

Investments (debit)	$50,000	
Unrealized Gain on Marketable Equity		
Securities (credit) (an equity account)		$50,000

After the $50,000 debit to the Investments account, that account would show a $180,000 debit balance. After the $50,000 credit, $80,000 would appear as unrealized gain in the equity section of the balance sheet. In addition, the $50,000 increase in the unrealized gain during Year 2 would appear in both "other comprehensive income" and comprehensive income. Although Vogt would not recognize any net income from the increase in fair value (again because no exchange transaction has occurred), the company's financial statements would show $50,000 in "other comprehensive income" and comprehensive income of $50,000 ($-0- net income plus $50,000 in "other comprehensive income").

When Vogt sells the Keller shares on February 1, Year 3, Vogt would record the following journal entry:

Cash (debit)	$170,000	
Unrealized Gain on Marketable Equity		
Securities (debit)	80,000	
Investments (credit)		$180,000
Gain on Sale of Investments (credit)		70,000

Because Vogt has sold its only investment, which appeared at $180,000 in the Investment account after the $80,000 increases in value during Years 1 and 2, Vogt can no longer show the unrealized gain as a separate item in shareholder's equity and must reverse the $80,000 that previously appeared as unrealized gain. Although Vogt can recognize $70,000 in gain, representing the difference between the $170,000 sales proceeds and the $100,000 original investment, the company must also report a ($80,000) (loss) in "other comprehensive income" from eliminating the balance in the unrealized gain account that appeared in shareholders' equity. Combined with the $70,000 in net income from the sale of investments, Vogt would report a ($10,000) (loss) in comprehensive income for Year 3.

We could summarize the effects on comprehensive income as follows:

	Net Income	Other Comprehensive Income	Comprehensive Income
Year 1	$-0-	$30,000	$30,000
Year 2	$-0-	$50,000	$50,000
Year 3	$70,000	($80,000)	($10,000)
Totals	$70,000	$-0-	$70,000

Note that all $70,000 in gain appears in net income during Year 3, while that same collective amount appears in comprehensive income over the same period as $30,000 income in Year 1, $50,000 income in Year 2, and a ($10,000) (loss) in Year 3. The requirement to report comprehensive income precludes an enterprise from recognizing all the income related to the increase in the value of an investment in the year of sale. Under the previous accounting rules, enterprises could decide when to recognize gains from investments (recall the Reliance Group Holdings case on pages 377-381).

5. Earnings Per Share

Page 489. Replace the discussion in the casebook with the following:

Recall from the discussion updating Chapter IV, *supra* at 47, that in 1997 the FASB issued FASB Statement No. 128, *Earnings Per Share*, to simplify the rules for computing earnings per share in financial statements for periods ending after December 15, 1997. As a result of these rules, enterprises with simple capital structures, meaning those with only common shares outstanding, must report basic per-share amounts for income from continuing operations and for net income on the face of the income statement. All other enterprises must present both basic and diluted per share amounts for income from continuing operations and for net income with equal prominence on the face of the income statement. Enterprises that report a discontinued operation, an extraordinary item, or the cumulative effect of a change in an accounting principle can present basic and diluted per share amounts for those line items either on the face of the income statement or in the notes to the financial statements. These rules apply to entities with publicly held common stock or outstanding contractual obligations, such as options, warrants or other securities, that would have allowed, or may allow, holders to obtain common stock either during, or after the end of, the reporting period and to other enterprises that choose to present earnings per share in the financial statements. Earnings per Share, Statement of Financial Accounting Standards No. 128, ¶¶ 6, 36, 37 (Financial Accounting Standards Bd. 1997).

E. Drafting and Negotiating Agreements and Legal Documents Containing Terminology Implicating the Income Statement

Page 497. Insert the following notes before the Problems:

1. Several commentators have recently discussed the movie industry's net profits accounting. *See, e.g.*, Victor P. Goldberg, *The Net Profits Puzzle*, 97 Colum. L. Rev. 524, 549-550 (1997) (concluding that net profits clauses give various participants incentives both during production and distribution); Tim Connors, Note, *Beleaguered Accounting: Should the Film Industry Abandon Its Net Profits Formula?*, 70 S. Cal.

L. Rev. 841, 916-919 (1997) (suggesting an alternative "comparison pool formula" for computing "net profit participation" payments under film industry contracts). Shortly before this supplement went to print, the AICPA issued a statement of position on accounting for motion picture production and distribution costs, effective for fiscal years beginning after December 15, 2000. Accounting by Producers or Distributors of Films, Statement of Position 00-2 (American Inst. of Certified Pub. Accountants 2000).

2. You may recall from the discussion in Chapter V that given the devastating effects that changes in accounting principles can cause in restrictive covenants and other legal documents, lawyers should try to stay abreast of the FASB's activities and agenda. With that suggestion in mind, we highlight several recent developments and areas to watch regarding the income statement.

(a) *Derivatives.* As described earlier, *supra* at 56-57, and effective for all quarters of fiscal years beginning after June 15, 2000, FASB Statement No. 133, Accounting for Derivative Instruments and Hedging Activities, requires enterprises to include the changes in the fair values of various derivatives contracts during an accounting period in either "net income" or "comprehensive income." Including these changes in value in the income statement obviously affects numerous financial ratios and could potentially cause, or cure, defaults in many contracts and lending agreements.

(b) *Comprehensive Income.* Now that FASB Statement No. 130 requires enterprises to report and display "comprehensive income" to reflect all nonowner changes in equity for fiscal years beginning after December 15, 1997, will or should "comprehensive income" replace the terms "income" or "net income" in various financial contracts? Do references to "income" or "net income" in existing contracts really mean "comprehensive income" as the new "bottom line?" For example, can management include increases in unrealized holding gains on securities when computing bonuses based upon a certain percentage of "income?" Can management exclude unrealized losses on derivatives contracts that only affect "comprehensive income?"

(c) *Earnings Per Share.* How will the new requirements in FASB Statement No. 128 that enterprises compute "basic earnings per share" and "diluted earnings per share" for fiscal periods ending after December 15, 1997 affect references to "primary earnings per share" and "fully diluted earnings per share" in previously existing contracts that do not address changes in generally accepted accounting principles? How should courts interpret contracts entered into after 1997 that use the old terms "primary earnings per share" or "fully diluted earnings per share?"

(d) *Consolidation policy.* Since 1982, albeit not full-time, the FASB has been working on new guidelines for enterprises to follow when deciding whether to consolidate the activities of subsidiaries or affiliates for financial reporting purposes. As you may recall from the discussion in the casebook on page 412, current accounting rules generally require consolidation if one enterprise owns more than fifty percent of the other entity's voting shares. This bright-line test, however, has allowed enterprises to use various techniques, such as maintaining fifty percent or less ownership, to avoid consolidating poorly-performing subsidiaries or reporting research and development expenses on the income statement. Under the revised proposal, a control test would trigger the consolidation requirement, which would continue to apply until the parent ceases to control the other enterprise. The proposed standard defines "control" as a nonshared decision-making ability of an entity to direct the policies and management that guide the ongoing activities of another entity so as to increase its benefits and limit its losses from that other entity's activities. Such changes could obviously affect an enterprise's balance sheet, income statement, and financial ratios and could potentially cause, or cure, defaults in many contracts and lending agreements.

CHAPTER VII

CONTINGENCIES

A. IMPORTANCE TO LAWYERS

Page 500. After the third sentence in the third paragraph on the bottom of the page, insert the following citations:

See, e.g., In re Corning, Inc. Securities Litigation, No. 92 Civ. 345 (TPG), 1997 WL 235122 (S.D.N.Y. May 7, 1997) (concluding that the consolidated and amended class action complaint sufficiently alleges that Corning's consolidated financial statements and periodic reports failed to reveal information about potential liabilities that a subsidiary, Dow Corning Corp., may have incurred in manufacturing and selling breast implants to approximately 800,000 women); Rehm v. Eagle Finance Corp., 954 F.Supp. 1246 (N.D. Ill. 1997) (denying defendants' motion to dismiss a complaint alleging that the defendant company and executive officers failed to follow GAAP in reporting credit losses from automobile and retail installment sales contracts with "sub-prime" consumers, thereby overstating earnings and artificially inflating stock prices).

Page 501. In the second sentence of the first full paragraph, add a reference to determining the legality of a corporate distribution and add the following citation at the end of the sentence.

See, e.g., Commonwealth Transp. Commissioner v. Matyiko, 253 Va. 1, 481 S.E.2d 468 (1997) (concluding that even though the corporation did not need to record a contingent liability in the financial statements, the directors could not vote to distribute all the corporation's assets to shareholders without making arrangements for the potential need to pay the liability and holding the directors personally liable when the liability materialized).

C. SECURITIES DISCLOSURE ISSUES

Page 523. At the bottom of the page, insert the following as note 1 and renumber existing note 1 as note 1A:

1. The SEC has entered cease-and-desist orders against at least one registrant and three individuals for failing to accrue and disclose estimated environmental cleanup costs in financial statements and periodic reports. As early as 1987, the registrant

learned about contamination in the company's soil and groundwater. Beginning the following year, a state water quality control board ("state board") repeatedly ordered the company to investigate the contamination. In 1991, upon learning that the registrant was not investigating, the Environmental Protection Agency ("EPA") designated the company as a potentially responsible party ("PRP"). By the end of its fiscal year, the company had received consultants' reports that confirmed contamination and another report from the company's own environmental consultant that estimated the company's environmental investigation and cleanup costs at $465,200. Nevertheless, the registrant failed to disclose the $465,200 estimate in its financial reports for the fiscal year and falsely reported that it was conducting further tests. In 1992, the company's chairman of the board sent a letter to the company's insurance carrier estimating environmental investigation and research costs at $700,000. In its periodic filing for 1992, however, the company falsely stated that the EPA had not designated it as a PRP, that the EPA had announced that the contamination was low enough that the agency would not currently require a cleanup, and that the company had no information about the cleanup costs for its property. The company also failed to disclose that it still had not completed the investigation that the state board had required. Even though both the state and county cited the company for improperly storing and discharging chemicals and hazardous waste in 1993, the company continued to deny its environmental obligations, made material false statements, and failed to disclose other material information, including EPA test results that showed that the contamination originated on the company's property, that the EPA had estimated total cleanup costs for the relevant portion of the Superfund site at $30 million, or that given the joint and several liability that potentially applies to PRPs, the company could incur at least a share of the $30 million in estimated cleanup costs, from 1993 to 1996. The SEC concluded that the company failed to accrue and disclose the estimated investigation and cleanup costs and therefore violated FASB Statement No. 5, FASB Interpretation No. 14 and SAB No. 92. In addition, the SEC concluded that the registrant used its periodic filings with the SEC during 1991 to 1996 to mislead investors about the company's environmental contamination, investigation, cleanup responsibilities and potential liabilities. In re Lee Pharmaceuticals, Accounting and Auditing Enforcement Release No. 1023, 7 Fed. Sec. L. Rep. (CCH) ¶ 74,538, 1998 WL 164350 (S.E.C.).

Page 526. At the end of note 3 near the bottom on the page, add the following notes about the use of required reports under the federal securities laws to obtain information about an opponent's assessment of pending litigation and proposed SEC rules that would require additional disclosures about loss accrual accounts from registrants:

4. After its 1994 bankruptcy, Orange County filed a lawsuit on January 12, 1995 seeking more than $2 billion from Merrill Lynch & Co., Inc. for the brokerage firm's role in the risky derivatives-based investment scheme that ultimately led to the nation's largest municipal bankruptcy. On June 2, 1998, Orange County and Merrill Lynch announced a $400 million settlement to end the lawsuit. In one of the ensuing press releases, Merrill Lynch "announced that it was fully reserved for the settlement and 'that the payment will have no financial impact on earnings reported in the 1998 second quarter or subsequent quarters.'" *Merrill Lynch to Pay $400 Million to Settle Orange County Bankruptcy Suit*, 30 Sec. Reg. & L. Rep. (BNA) 846 (1998). A close examination of the supplemental table for "Non-Interest Expenses" in the MD&A in Merrill Lynch's Form 10-K for the fiscal year ended December 27, 1996 (filed March 21, 1997) reveals that other non-interest expenses increased from $697 million in fiscal 1995 to $859 million in fiscal 1996. At the very end of the textual discussion in that section, the following statement appears: "Other expenses rose 23% due in part to provisions related to various business activities and goodwill amortization." The same supplemental table in the MD&A in Merrill Lynch's Form 10-K for the fiscal year ended December 26, 1997 (filed March 3, 1998) also reveals that other non-interest expenses increased from $859 million in fiscal 1996 to $1,136 million in fiscal 1997. At the end of the third paragraph in textual discussion for that section, the MD&A comments: "Other expenses increased 32% from 1996 due to increases in provisions for various business activities and legal matters, and higher office and postage costs." The very last sentence in that section repeats the statement that appeared in the 1996 MD&A: "Other expenses rose 23% due in part to provisions related to various business activities and goodwill amortization." As counsel for Orange County would you find this information helpful? How might you use those disclosures to gather additional information, financial or other, that might help your client?

In similar fashion and without admitting any wrongdoing, Merrill Lynch agreed in May 2000 to pay Sumitomo Corp. $275 million and legal fees to settle a lawsuit that sought to recover about $1.7 billion in losses that Sumitomo suffered during a 1996 copper trading scandal. Again, Merrill Lynch announced that the settlement would "not have a material impact on earnings reported in the second quarter of 2000." Barry Hall, *Merrill to Pay Sumitomo $275 Million To Avoid Suit Over '96 Copper Scandal*, 32 Sec. Reg. & L. Rep. (BNA) 753, 754 (2000). *See also* Bruce Orwall, *Observers Say Disney-Katzenberg Spat Could Have Been Settled Sooner for Less*, Wall. St. J., July 9, 1999, at B3; Bruce Orwall, *A Conclusion In the Clash of Hollywood Titans*, Wall St. J., July 8, 1999, at B1 (collectively reporting that Walt Disney Co. agreed to pay an undisclosed amount exceeding $250 million to settle Jeffrey Katzenberg's breach of contract lawsuit against the company and stating that "Disney told Wall Street analysts that it has reserved for the amount of the settlement, which will have no impact on its earnings.")

A more modest illustration suggests that the Internal Revenue Service recently failed to review publicly available financial statements before resolving a tax dispute with Wabash National Corporation ("Wabash"), a company that designs, manufactures and markets truck trailers and whose shares trade on the New York Stock Exchange. In the notes to Wabash's financial statements in the company's Form 10-K for the fiscal year ended December 31, 1999, the following discussion appears in note 14 on commitments and contingencies:

On December 24, 1998, the Company received a notice from the Internal Revenue Service that it intended to assess federal excise tax on certain used trailers restored by the Company during 1996 and 1997. Although the Company strongly disagreed with the IRS, it recorded a $4.6 million accrual in 1998 for this loss contingency in Other, net in the accompanying Consolidated Statements of Income. During 1999 the Company reached a settlement with the IRS of approximately $1.1 million, net of interest, of which less than $1.0 million was related to the restoration of used trailers. Accordingly, during the fourth quarter 1999 the Company reflected a $3.5 million reversal in Other, net in the accompanying Consolidated Statements of Income.

Wabash National Corp., FORM 10-K, ANNUAL REPORT PURSUANT TO SECTION 13 OR 15(d) OF THE SECURITIES EXCHANGE ACT OF 1934, at 39 (for the fiscal year ended December 31, 1999) (filed Mar. 29, 2000). The related MD&A reveals that in December 1999 Wabash favorably resolved the dispute for less than twenty-five percent of the accrued amount, or for approximately $1.1 million, net of interest, of which less than $1 million related to the restoration of used trailers. As a result, Wabash eliminated the remaining accrual, thereby recognizing $3.5 million in other income in December 1999. *Id.* at 14. Interestingly, the parallel note on commitments and contingencies to Wabash's financial statements for the year ended December 31, 1998 provided in pertinent part:

> On December 24, 1998, the Company received notice from the Internal Revenue Service that it intends to assess federal excise tax on certain used trailers restored by the Company during 1996 and 1997. The Company strongly disagrees with and intends to vigorously contest the assessment. In applying generally accepted accounting principles, the Company recorded a $4.6 million accrual in 1998 for this loss contingency that is reflected in Other, net in the accompanying Consolidated Statements of Income. The Company continued the restoration program with the same customer during 1998. The customer has indemnified the Company for any potential excise tax assessed by the IRS for years subsequent to 1997. As a result, the Company has recorded a liability and a corresponding receivable of $2.4 million for 1998 in the accompanying Consolidated Balance Sheets.

Wabash National Corp., FORM 10-K, ANNUAL REPORT PURSUANT TO SECTION 13 OR 15(d) OF THE SECURITIES EXCHANGE ACT OF 1934, at 41 (for the fiscal year ended December 31, 1998) (filed Mar. 31, 1999). As counsel for the Internal Revenue Service, how might you have used that information? As counsel for Wabash, how might you respond to any such efforts? Might any other facts or legal arguments better explain this settlement?

5.   In January 2000, the SEC proposed to amend Regulation S-K to require registrants to provide supplemental financial information about changes in each major class of loss accrual accounts, including liabilities for environmental costs, contingent income tax liabilities, product warranty liabilities, and probable losses from pending litigation. The supplemental information would include the beginning balance by major class of account, additions charged to expense during the fiscal period, deductions or other additions, and the ending balance in the category. The

proposed instructions specifically state that "[a]ll loss contingencies recorded pursuant to the requirements of FASB Statement 5 should be reported." Supplementary Financial Information, 65 Fed. Reg. 4585 (2000) (proposed Jan. 31, 2000 to be codified at 17 C.F.R. § 229.302(c)). Both litigators and transactional lawyers should monitor the status of these proposed rules carefully.

D. AUDIT INQUIRIES AND RELEVANT PROFESSIONAL STANDARDS

Page 534. Insert the following note 1A before note 2:

1A. In an attempt to preserve the attorney-client privilege regarding unasserted possible claims or assessments, some lawyers refuse to respond to general inquiries relating to the existence of such items in auditors' requests for information. In a recent interpretation, the Auditing Standards Board concluded that such refusals do not thereby limit the scope of the audit. The ASB, however, reiterated that the lawyer should confirm the assumption underlying the understanding between the legal and accounting professions that the lawyer, under certain circumstances, will advise the client concerning the client's obligation to make financial statement disclosures regarding unasserted possible claims or assessments. Use of Explanatory Language Concerning Unasserted Possible Claims or Assessments in Lawyers' Responses to Audit Inquiry Letters, Auditing Interpretation No. 10 of Section 337 (Auditing Standards Bd. 1997), codified at American Institute of Certified Public Accountants, 1 Professional Standards (CCH) AU § 9337.31-.32 (Feb. 1997).

E. DISCOVERY ISSUES

1. AUDIT INQUIRY LETTERS

Page 545. At the end of note 1 at the top of the page, add the following paragraph:

Not all courts have adopted the "primarily to assist in pending or impending litigation" standard espoused in *United States v. Gulf Oil Corporation, supra* at 542, when applying the work product doctrine. In United States v. Adlman, 134 F.3d 1194 (2nd Cir. 1998), the Second Circuit recently rejected that test and instead applied a "because of" standard that has been used in the Third, Fourth, Eighth, and D.C. Circuits. Under this "because of" formulation, the work product doctrine protects documents that "'can fairly be said to have been prepared or obtained because of the prospect of litigation.'" Id. at 1202 (quoting Charles Alan Wright, Arthur R. Miller & Richard L. Marcus, 8 Federal Practice & Procedure § 2024, at 343 (1994). Under this latter standard, a document does not lose the protection under the work product doctrine merely because the document was created to assist with a business decision. In dicta, however, the *Adlman* court observed that the "because of" formulation would withhold work product protection from "documents that are prepared in the ordinary course of business or that would have been created in essentially similar form irrespective of the litigation." Even in such circumstances, however, under Rule 26(b)(3) of the Federal Rules of Civil Procedure, the district court retains "the authority to protect against disclosure of the mental impressions, strategies, and analyses of the party or its representative concerning the litigation." *Id.* at 1202-03.

A recent law review article offers a helpful insight into the *Adlman* decision's potential significance. The authors posit that the work product doctrine has historically protected most of the materials that litigators produce. In contrast, the legal work that corporate or transactional lawyers produce typically has not merited the same degree of protection. In their view, the Second Circuit's decision "threatens to disrupt this traditional dichotomy." Charles M. Yablon & Steven S. Sparling, *United States v. Adlman: Protection for Corporate Work Product*, 64 Brook. L. Rev. 627 (1998) (also exploring the work product doctrine's potential availability to lawyers and other persons engaged in business and tax planning; preparing financial statements, disclosures under the federal securities laws, or responses to audit inquiry letters; drafting transactional documents; or performing other tasks in a corporate legal department).

Page 545. At the end of the first paragraph in note 3, add the following:

More recently, Judge John Martin of the same court granted in significant part a motion to compel that plaintiffs in a securities fraud case pending in federal court in Florida and involving Sensormatic Electronics Corp. filed against third party Willkie Farr & Gallagher, a leading New York law firm. The motion to compel sought certain documents relating to an investigation that the law firm conducted on behalf of Sensormatic's audit committee. The audit committee had disclosed the results of the investigation to Ernst & Young, the company's auditing firm, to obtain an unqualified audit opinion. The court held that this disclosure waived the attorney-client privilege. In re Subpoena Duces Tecum Served on Willke Farr & Gallagher, No. M8-85 (JSM), 1997 WL 118369 (S.D.N.Y. Mar. 14, 1997).

2. Accountant-Client Privilege

Page 547. Replace the third sentence in the introductory paragraph with the following:

Although the IRS Restructuring and Reform Bill of 1998 creates an accountant-client privilege in civil tax matters before the Internal Revenue Service or in federal courts, the legislation will not protect accountant-client communications from disclosure in other contexts and does not change the "ability of any other body, including the [SEC], to gain or compel information." Conf. Rep. to accompany H.R. 2676, 105th Cong., 2d Sess. 88 (as released on June 24, 1998); *see also IRS Reform Law Creates New Privilege Between Taxpayers, Tax Practitioners*, Corp. Counsel Weekly, Aug. 12,

1998, at 3; Elizabeth MacDonald, *IRS Bill Gives Accountants New Privileges*, Wall St. J., June 26, 1998, at A4.

Page 547. After the citation to the Wright and Graham treatise on Federal Practice and Procedure in the introductory paragraph, add the following:

A very recent decision of the Supreme Court of Colorado notes that "[a]t least thirty states have codified some form of protection for communications between an accountant and a client." Colorado State Board of Accountancy v. Zaveral Boosalis Raisch, 960 P.2d 102, 106 n.3 (Colo. 1998) (listing applicable statutes).

Page 556. Add the following to the end of note 2:

A recent law review note suggests that the recognition of a federal psychotherapist-patient privilege in *Jaffee v. Redmond*, 518 U.S. 1, 116 S.Ct. 1923, 135 L.Ed.2d 337 (1996), opens the door to new arguments that the federal judiciary should recognize an accountant-client privilege in federal matters. The article, however, ultimately concludes that even under the new and broader approach to granting privileges espoused in the recent decision, the federal system will not recognize an accountant-client privilege until more states recognize meaningful accountant-client privileges. Thomas J. Molony, Note, *Is the Supreme Court Ready to Recognize Another Privilege? An Examination of the Accountant-Client Privilege in the Aftermath of Jaffee v. Redmond*, 55 Wash. & Lee L. Rev. 247 (1998).

Page 557. At the end of the first paragraph of note 5, insert the following citation:

United States v. Massachusetts Inst. of Tech., 129 F.3d 681 (1st Cir. 1997) (holding that MIT forfeited both the attorney-client privilege and work product protection by disclosing documents sought by the Internal Revenue Service to the Defense Contract Audit Agency, the auditing arm of the Department of Defense, during a performance review on certain defense contracts and joining five other circuits, out of the six other circuits that have considered the question, in concluding that earlier disclosure at the request of government agency destroys the privilege).

Page 557. Insert the following case at the beginning of the citation at the end of the second full paragraph in note 5.

United States v. Massachusetts Inst. of Tech., *supra* at 687 (listing five circuits that have adopted the rule that disclosure to a non-adversary does not waive work product protection, restating the prevailing rule as "disclosure to an adversary, real or potential, forfeits work product protection," and treating the disclosure to the Defense Contract Audit Agency as disclosure to a potential adversary).

Page 559. In note 7, insert the following citation after the reference to the Simon v. G.D. Searle & Co. case near the middle of the page:

General Electric Capital Corp. v. DirectTV, Inc., 184 F.R.D. 32 (D. Conn. 1998) (drawing a distinction between individual case reserves and aggregate figures and concluding, after in camera review, that five documents pertaining to defendants' loss reserves were both relevant and not privileged under either the work-product doctrine or the attorney-client privilege).

Page 559. In note 7, insert the following discussion before the last sentence:

Finally, dicta from at least one court suggests that information about litigation reserves might even qualify as admissible evidence. In *In re Amino Acid Lysine Antitrust Litigation*, 1996 WL 197671 (N.D. Ill. Apr. 22, 1996), Senior District Judge Shadur ordered disclosure of any reserves that defendant Archer-Daniels-Midland Company had established for the underlying antitrust litigation before the court would rule that the proposed settlement in the class action fell within the range of fairness, reasonableness and adequacy. The judge wrote: "In this Court's experience in representing public companies, or in separately representing the outside directors of public companies, it has found such reserves to be a material indicium of the fair value of a liability, estimated by those who are presumably in the best position to make such an evaluation." *Id*. at *5.

CHAPTER VIII

INVENTORY

B. DETERMINING ENDING INVENTORY

1. WHICH COSTS AND GOODS TO INCLUDE IN INVENTORY

a. INCLUDABLE COSTS

(2) Manufacturer

Page 575. After note 2, insert the following new note:

3. In 1984, Congress created foreign sales corporations ("FSCs") to offer tax incentives to stimulate U.S. exports and reduce the trade deficit. A recent article concludes that tax literature and exporters have largely overlooked the tax savings that result if FSCs use marginal costing. Fred A. Jacobs & Ernest R. Larkins, *Export Tax Incentives for Establishing Foreign Markets: An Analysis of Marginal Costing Techniques*, 12 Acct. Horizons 374 (1998).

(3) Other Illustrations of "Cost Accounting"

Page 582. At the end of note 5, insert the following:

See also Lynn McGuire, Note, *Federal Research Grant Funding at Universities: Legislative Waves From Auditors Diving Into Overhead Cost Pools*, 23 J.C. & U.L. 563 (1997).

6. Cost allocation issues also arise under the Medicare reimbursement regulations. In 1998, federal investigators launched a fraud probe against Beverly Enterprises, Inc. for allegedly violating those regulations and improperly and inequitably allocating certain nursing labor costs between the Medicare certified and non-certified units, exposing the company to possible fines reportedly totaling more than $300 million. Various shareholders in the company responded by filing a securities fraud class action against the company and several senior officers. *Investors File Suit Against Beverly Enterprises Alleging Medicare Fraud*, 30 Sec. Reg. & L. Rep.(BNA) 1506 (1998).

b. WHAT ITEMS TO COUNT AS INVENTORY

Page 587. Add to the end of the first full paragraph:

Antar's guilty plea to the racketeering conspiracy charges eventually led to his sentence to a federal prison term of eighty-two months, plus supervised release for an additional two years. *'Crazy Eddie' Antar Sentenced To 82 Months On Racketeering Charges*, 29 Sec. Reg. & L. Rep. (BNA) 190 (1997).

2. HOW TO PRICE INVENTORY ITEMS

b. LOWER OF COST OR MARKET

Page 618. Add to note 1:

As an example of another recent case involving the accounting treatment of inventories, see *Novak v. Kasaks*, 997 F. Supp. 425 (S.D.N.Y. 1998) (dismissing a complaint that alleged that AnnTaylor Stores Corporation, a wholly-owned subsidiary, and certain officers and directors participated in a "box-and-hold" scheme in which the retailer hid excess inventory in warehouses and failed to write-down inventory at the proper times on the ground that the complaint did not satisfy the requirements for pleading scienter under the Private Securities Litigation Reform Act of 1995).

CHAPTER IX

LONG-LIVED ASSETS AND INTANGIBLES

A. IMPORTANCE TO LAWYERS

Page 631. At the end of the first paragraph at the top of the page, insert the following discussion:

In a 1998 speech at the NYU Center for Law and Business, *supra* at 63-69, SEC Chairman Arthur Levitt announced an action plan to combat accounting "illusions," including "'big bath' restructuring charges" and "creative acquisition accounting," which the Chairman also referred to as "merger magic." Under this latter technique, you may recall that acquiring companies increasingly treat large portions of the total consideration paid to acquire a target as purchasing "in-process research and development." See *supra* at 65-66. Because accounting rules in this country require enterprises to treat all research and development costs as expenses in the period incurred, acquirors then immediately writeoff these in-process research and development charges.

Page 631. After the third bullet point, insert the following:

• The Gartner Group, an international information technology advisory and market research firm, estimated that entities would spend between $300 and $600 billion to correct Year 2000 problems. Year 2000 Task Force, The Year 2000 Issue[:] Current Accounting and Auditing Guidance (American Inst. of Certified Pub. Accountants 1997). How should financial statements report such costs?

• As the Internet emerges, enterprises have spent, and will continue to spend, enormous amounts to develop the content and the graphics on their Web sites. How should firms treat these costs for financial accounting purposes?

B. CLASSIFICATION OF EXPENDITURES: ASSETS VS. EXPENSES

Pages 643. After the carryover paragraph in note 2 at the top of the page, insert the following:

Based on a provision in FASB Interpretation No. 4, *Applicability of FASB Statement No. 2 to Business Combinations Accounted for by the Purchase Method, an interpretation of FASB Statement No. 2* (1975), that requires an enterprise immediately to expense goodwill attributed to in-process research and development in certain circumstances, acquiring companies have increasingly treated large portions of the total consideration paid to acquire a target as purchasing "in-process research and development" and then immediately written off these charges. Observers have noted the irony inherent in the current rules that recognize in-process research development as an asset, require acquiring enterprises to measure the intangible asset's value, and then obliterate the intangible from the balance sheet. Baruch Lev, a NYU professor, has reportedly described this accounting treatment as "flash, then flush." Noting that charges for in-process research and development during 1998 rose to 247 instances totaling $19.6 billion, the SEC staff has been carefully reviewing these writeoffs. During a one year period in the late 1990s, the SEC investigated about $10 billion of the charges and forced companies to reclassify $5 billion. In the words of Lynn Turner, the agency's Chief Accountant, the SEC has challenged valuations of purchased research and development "when the amounts assigned are disconnected from reality." America Online, for example, reportedly needed to postpone the release of its fiscal 1998 earnings from early August until late September so that the company could settle an accounting dispute with the SEC's staff on this subject. As part of its action plan to address concerns about earnings management, the SEC notified more than 150 publicly traded companies that the staff may review their 1998 annual reports for various issues, including charges related to acquired research and development. Steve Burkholder, *FASB Proposes End to Instant Write-offs Of 'in-Process R&D' in Acquisitions*, 31 Sec. Reg. & L. Rep. (BNA) 289 (1999); Steve Burkholder, *SEC Notifies 150-Plus Companies Of Possible Review of Write-Downs Reporting*, 31 Sec. Reg. & L. Rep. (BNA) 153 (1999); Steve Burkholder, *SEC Warns 'In-Process R&D' Writeoffs In Mergers Could Lead to Restatements*, 30 Sec. Reg. & L. Rep. (BNA) 1454 (1998).

Page 643. Insert the following note 2A before note 3:

2A. Several recent accounting pronouncements supply new guidance as to whether enterprises should immediately charge various costs against current earnings or treat them as capital expenditures in efforts to eliminate inconsistencies in financial reporting. *See, e.g.*, Reporting on the Costs of Start-Up Activities, Statement of Position 98-5 (American Inst. of Certified Pub. Accountants 1998) (mandating businesses to expense organization costs and costs related to start-up activities as incurred for fiscal periods beginning after December 15, 1998); Accounting for the Costs of Computer Software Developed or Obtained for Internal Use, Statement of Position 98-1 (American Inst. of Certified Pub. Accountants 1998) (for financial statements for fiscal years beginning after December 15, 1998, requiring enterprises to expense, as incurred, computer software costs incurred in preliminary project stages, similar costs stemming from research and development, training costs, maintenance costs, and many costs related to data conversion, while specifying capitalization for external direct costs of materials and services used to develop or acquire internal use software, payroll costs for employees who work directly on tasks related to the internal use software, and interest costs incurred while developing such software); Accounting for Web Site Development Costs, Emerging Issues Task Force

Issue No. 00-2 (Emerging Issues Task Force, Financial Accounting Standards Bd. 2000) (concluding that enterprises should capitalize initial development costs for Web graphics, but can expense changes to the graphics); Accounting for Costs Incurred in Connection with a Consulting Contract or Internal Project That Combines Business Process Reengineering and Information Technology Transformation, Emerging Issues Task Force Issue No. 97-13 (Emerging Issues Task Force, Financial Accounting Standards Bd. 1997) (generally requiring enterprises to record such costs as expenses).

E. INTANGIBLES

2. UNIDENTIFIABLE INTANGIBLES

a. BUSINESS COMBINATIONS

(3) Comparison of the Pooling and Purchase Methods

Page 680. At the end of the last full paragraph, add the following citation:

For a recent article which discusses and describes pooling as "probably the most notorious example" of situations where companies select a particular accounting method or enter into a particular business transaction to improve their financial appearance, see Claire A. Hill, *Why Financial Appearances Might Matter: An Explanation for "Dirty Pooling" and Some Other Types of Financial Cosmetics*, 22 Del. J. Corp. L. 141, 144, 161-163 (1997).

Page 681. At the end of the first full paragraph, add the following example:

Another recent transaction further illustrates the significant differences in accounting treatment between the pooling and purchase methods, albeit not in the context of a hostile take-over. Because Daimler-Benz A.G. had already become one of the first German companies to use U.S. accounting rules, the recent merger between that company and Chrysler Corporation qualified for pooling. As a result, the auto companies avoided recording more than $20 billion in goodwill, which would have reduced the new company's earnings by at least $500 million annually for the next forty years. Melody Petersen, *Market Place[:] An accounting method favored in mergers may get a new name*, N.Y. Times, May 13, 1998, at D8.

b. GOODWILL

Page 697. Following the first full paragraph, insert the following notes:

7. For recent discussions about valuations, see Robert B. Dickie, FINANCIAL STATEMENT ANALYSIS AND BUSINESS VALUATION FOR THE PRACTICAL LAWYER (1998);

Jay W. Eisenhofer & John L. Reed, *Valuation Litigation*, 22 Del. J. Corp. L. 37 (1997) (presenting an overview of selected valuation methodologies and discussing how valuation disputes arise in various contexts; the legal standards that apply to such claims; the different financial standards that courts have applied to the actual valuation calculations in the different proceedings; and adjustments for various discounts and control premium); and Gene A. Trevino, *A Note on Formulating and Corroborating Discount Rates for Small Firms*, 7 J. Leg. Econ. 45 (1998) (discussing the formulation of an appropriate discount rate for small firms, such as sole proprietorships, with annual sales less than $1 million).

8. Continuing earlier discussions about the various ways that changes in accounting principles can cause violations of restrictive covenants and accelerate contractual obligations, we again highlight several topics on the FASB's agenda:

(a) Business combinations. The FASB has tentatively decided to eliminate future use of the advantageous pooling of interests method and to require purchase accounting in future business combinations. During their discussions, board members have highlighted the importance of information about an acquisition's real price and performance over time to investors. If this tentative decision leads to a final pronouncement, the FASB would adopt standards similar to rules and practices outside the United States, where the purchase method predominates. In September 1999, the FASB issued an exposure draft on this topic. Business Combinations and Intangible Assets, Proposed Statement of Financial Accounting Standards (Financial Accounting Standards Bd. 1999).

(b) Goodwill. As part of its ongoing business combinations project, the FASB has tentatively decided that an acquiring company should continue to record goodwill as an asset on the balance sheet. Unlike the existing rules that allow for up to a forty-year amortization period for purchased goodwill, however, the Board has tentatively proposed new treatment that would cut the maximum amortization period in half to twenty years. Business Combinations and Intangible Assets, Proposed Statement of Financial Accounting Standards (Financial Accounting Standards Bd. 1999).

The FASB has also tentatively proposed to change the rules for negative goodwill, which generally arises from either a bargain purchase or when difficult meshing of the separate activities of the participants in a business combination impose negative synergies, and which admittedly affects very few business combinations. Rather than amortizing this negative goodwill by increasing income over a period which may not exceed forty years as the current rules require, the Board has tentatively decided that the acquirer should immediately recognize the entire negative goodwill as an extraordinary gain. Business Combinations and Intangible Assets, Proposed Statement of Financial Accounting Standards (Financial Accounting Standards Bd. 1999).

(c) Purchased in-process research and development. Even before SEC Chairman Arthur Levitt highlighted "merger magic" as one of five "illusions" in current accounting practice, *supra* at 65-66, the FASB had begun to consider additional standards on accounting for purchased intangibles, including purchased in-process research and development. As a second phase in the FASB's business combinations project, the FASB plans to study purchased research and development as part of a wider project on research and development costs. The FASB, however, does not expect to devote any significant effort on that project until at least 2001. The AICPA has also established a special working group on the issue. Steve Burkholder, *FASB Continues Rulemaking Process For Business Combinations Accounting*, 32 Sec. Reg. & L. Rep. (BNA) 166 (2000).

F. LEASE ACCOUNTING

1. CLASSIFICATION

Page 699. At the end of the first full paragraph on the page, insert the following:

The FASB recently released a codification, as of October 1, 1998, of the various lease accounting pronouncements, including the full text of Emerging Issues Task Force abstracts related to leases. The 450 page publication, entitled "Accounting for Leases," includes a CD-ROM that allows electronic searches. Steve Burkholder, *FASB Updates and Expands Lease Accounting Publication*, 31 Sec. Reg. & L. Rep. (BNA) 46 (1999); Steve Burkholder, *SEC Warns 'In-Process R&D' Writeoffs In Mergers Could Lead to Restatements*, 30 Sec. Reg. & L. Rep. (BNA) 1454 (1998).

2. TREATMENT

Page 703. After Problem 9.7C on the bottom of the page, insert the following new section:

3. SYNTHETIC LEASES

In recent years, the term "synthetic lease" has come to refer to arrangements which qualify as an operating lease for financial accounting purposes, but which function as conditional sales for federal and state income tax, bankruptcy and commercial purposes. As operating leases for financial accounting purposes, the "lessee" can expense the rental payments and such transactions do not create new debt or cause an asset to appear on the "lessee's" balance sheet. For these latter reasons, such transactions may not trigger restrictive covenants in various lending agreements that might otherwise limit the "lessee's" ability to incur indebtedness. As conditional sales for other purposes, the "lessee" retains all the tax benefits arising from ownership, including the ability to depreciate the property and to deduct interest paid. In addition, the "lessee" can keep any appreciation upon a subsequent purchase of the property from the "lessor" or upon resale to a third party. These transactions raise significant accounting, antitrust, bankruptcy, commercial, disclosure, environmental, insurance, securities and tax issues. *See* John C. Murray,

Off-Balance-Sheet Financing: Synthetic Leases, 32 Real Prop. Prob. & Tr. J. 193 (1997).

G. WRITE-DOWNS AND THE "BIG BATH"

1. THE PROBLEM

Page 704. At the end of the last full sentence near the bottom of the page, insert the following:

Following AOL's announcement, disappointed investors filed a class action lawsuit against the company, alleging that the company and its officers violated federal securities laws. In June 1998, the company agreed to pay up to $35 million to settle the lawsuit, noting that insurance would cover a substantial portion of the settlement. Eric Auchard, *AOL to Settle Investor Suit for $35 Million*, Wash. Post, June 12, 1998, at F3; *Class Action Against AOL Alleges Insider Trading, Misstated Earnings*, 29 Sec. Reg. & L. Rep. (BNA) 282 (1997). More recently, AOL consented to a cease-and-desist order and agreed to pay a $3.5 million civil penalty to resolve administrative proceedings alleging that the company improperly accounted for its advertising costs. The company did not admit or deny the charges. SEC v. America Online, Inc., Accounting and Auditing Enforcement Release No. 1258, 7 Fed. Sec. L. Rep. (CCH) ¶ _____ (May 15, 2000).

Page 705. At the end of the first full paragraph at the top of the page, insert the following:

More recently, *The New York Times* reported that a researcher who studies accounting issues tracked 1,400 restructuring charges totaling $76 billion in 1998. Louis Uchitelle, *Corporate Profits Are Tasty, But Artificially Flavored*, N.Y. Times, Mar. 28, 1999, sec. B, at 4. Investor Warren Buffet has compared the financial statements that follow these writeoffs to bogus golf scores. Imagine a golfer reporting an atrociously high score for his first round, say a 140, and then shooting in the eighties "for the next few rounds by drawing down against the 'reserve' established in the first round. 'On Wall Street, * * * they will ignore the 140--which after all, came from a "discontinued" swing--and will classify our hero as an 80 shooter (and one who never disappoints.)'" Richard A. Oppel Jr., *Buffet Deplores Trend of Manipulated Earnings*, N.Y. Times, Mar. 15, 1999, at C2.

The SEC staff has been carefully reviewing such writeoffs and has challenged several registrants' attempted writeoffs. *See, e.g.*, Seth Schiesel, *S.E.C. Is Challenging MCI On Accounting Procedures*, N.Y. Times, Apr. 2, 1998, at D2 (reporting that the SEC had questioned $752 million in charges that the company took against earnings in its 1997 fourth quarter, which resulted in a $391 million loss for the period and a mere $2 million in profit for the year); Jeff Bailey, *Waste Management Discloses the SEC Has Begun Probe Into Its Bookkeeping*, Wall St. J.,

Mar. 31, 1998, at A6 (reporting that the trash hauler's $3.54 billion in charges and restated financial results back to 1991 arose from reducing the previously estimated capacity of its 130 garbage dumps, and shortening depreciation periods for trash trucks and other equipment); Michael Bologna, *Waste Hauling Firm, Arthur Andersen Reach $220 Million Settlement with Shareholders*, 30 Sec. Reg. & L. Rep. (BNA) 1738 (1998) (subsequently reporting that Waste Management and Arthur Andersen had tentatively agreed to pay $220 million to settle fifteen consolidated class action lawsuits). As part of its action plan to address concerns about earnings management, the SEC notified more than 150 publicly traded companies that the staff may review their 1998 annual reports for various issues, including restructuring charges. Steve Burkholder, *SEC Notifies 150-Plus Companies Of Possible Review of Write-Downs Reporting*, 31 Sec. Reg. & L. Rep. (BNA) 153 (1999).

2. The New Rules

Page 706. At the end of the carryover paragraph at the top of the page, insert the following discussion:

Staff accountants at the SEC have questioned the way that registrants are reporting restructuring and asset impairments charges and have suggested that firms are recognizing losses prematurely. Restructuring and Impairment Charges, Staff Accounting Bulletin No. 100, 64 Fed. Reg. 67,154 (1999), reprinted in 7 Fed. Sec. L. Rep. (CCH) ¶¶ 75,705, 75,721 at 64,227-3, 64,228, 64,269-70, 64,291-96 (Dec. 8, 1999). The FASB continues to work on an exposure draft to amend FASB Statement No. 121. The Board's tentative decisions would establish a single accounting model for all disposals of long-lived assets for obligations related to such disposal activities. As a result, the Board plans to expand FASB Statement No. 121's scope to apply to those disposals of segments of a business that APB Opinion No. 30, Reporting the Results of Operations-Reporting the Effects of Disposal of a Segment of a Business, and Extraordinary, Unusual and Infrequently Occurring Events and Transactions, currently covers. The draft rules will probably require future expenses arising from a plan to sell or abandon a fixed asset, such as a factory, to meet the definition of a liability before an enterprise can recognize them for financial accounting purposes. Such an amendment would limit enterprises' ability to record large up-front writedowns and would require firms to recognize such costs as actually incurred. Steve Burkholder, *FASB Advances Toward Proposed Changes, Guidance on Asset Impairment Accounting*, 32 Sec. Reg. & L. Rep. (BNA) 309 (2000).

APPENDIX

EXCERPTS FROM THE 1999 FORM 10-K FOR BEN & JERRY'S HOMEMADE, INC.*

FORM 10-K

SECURITIES AND EXCHANGE COMMISSION

Washington, D.C. 20549

[X]ANNUAL REPORT PURSUANT TO SECTION 13 OR 15(d) OF

THE SECURITIES EXCHANGE ACT OF 1934

For the fiscal year ended December 25, 1999

[ ]TRANSITION REPORT PURSUANT TO SECTION 13 OR 15(d)
OF THE SECURITIES EXCHANGE ACT OF 1934

For the transition period from _____ to _____

Commission File Number 0-13544

BEN & JERRY'S HOMEMADE, INC.

(Exact name of registrant as specified in its charter)

Vermont   03-0267543
(State of incorporation)   (I.R.S. Employer Identification No.)

30 Community Drive
South Burlington, Vermont   05403-6828
(Address of principal executive offices)   (Zip Code)

Registrant's telephone number, including area code: 802/846-1500

Securities registered pursuant to Section 12 (b) of the Act: None

Securities registered pursuant to Section 12 (g) of the Act:

Class A Common Stock, $.033 par value per share

Class B Common Stock, $.033 par value per share

Indicate by check mark whether the registrant (1) has filed all reports required to be filed by Section 13 or 15 (d) of the Securities Exchange Act of 1934 during the preceding 12 months (or for such shorter period that the registrant was required to file such reports), and (2) has been subject to such filing requirements for the past 90 days.

Yes X No _____

Indicate by check mark if disclosure of delinquent filers pursuant to Item 405 of Regulation S-K (225.405) is not contained herein, and will not be contained, to the best of registrant's knowledge, in definitive proxy or information statements incorporated by reference in Part III of this Form 10-K or any amendment to this Form 10-K.

[X]

The aggregate market value of the Company's Class A and Class B Common Stock held by non-affiliates was approximately $150,370,950 and $5,061,769 respectively, at February 25, 2000.

At February 25, 2000, 6,121,493 shares of the Company's Class A Common Stock and 794,539 shares of the Company's Class B Common Stock were outstanding.

* * *

*Used with permission of Ben & Jerry's Homemade Holdings, Inc. 2000

BEN & JERRY'S HOMEMADE, INC.

1999 FORM 10-K ANNUAL REPORT

Table of Contents

ITEM 1.   BUSINESS

Introduction

Ben & Jerry's Homemade, Inc. ("Ben & Jerry's" or the "Company") is a leading manufacturer of super premium ice cream, frozen yogurt and sorbet in unique and regular flavors. The Company also manufactures ice cream novelty products. The Company is committed to using milk and cream that have not been treated with the synthetic hormone, rBGH. The Company uses natural ingredients in its products. The Company embraces a philosophy that manifests itself in these attributes: being real and "down to earth," being humorous and having fun, being non-traditional and alternative and, at times, being activists around progressive values.

The Company's products are currently distributed throughout the United States primarily through independent distributors. However, the Company's marketing resources are concentrated on certain "target markets" including New England, New York, the Mid-Atlantic region, Florida, Texas, the West Coast and selected other major markets, including the Midwest (defined for this purpose as Chicago, Illinois, Minnesota, Wisconsin and Michigan) and Denver areas. In 1999, approximately 77% of the sales of the Company's packaged pints were attributable to these target markets. The Company's products are also available in certain "non-target" markets in the United States, the United Kingdom, France, Israel, Canada, The Netherlands, Belgium, Japan, Singapore, Peru and Lebanon. The Company currently markets flavors of its ice cream, frozen yogurt and sorbet in packaged pints, for sale primarily in supermarkets, other grocery stores, convenience stores and other retail food outlets and in bulk, primarily to restaurants and Ben & Jerry's company-owned franchised "scoop shops."

The Company began active operations in May 1978, when Jerry Greenfield, now the Company's Chairperson, and Ben Cohen, now the Company's Vice Chairperson, opened a retail store in a renovated gas station in Burlington, Vermont. The Company believes that it has maintained a reputation for producing gourmet-quality natural ice cream and frozen desserts, and for sponsoring or creating light-hearted promotions that foster an image as an independent socially conscious Vermont company.

The Board of Directors of the Company has since 1988 formalized its basic business philosophy by adopting a three-part "mission statement" for Ben & Jerry's. The statement includes a "product mission," "to make, distribute and sell the finest quality all natural ice cream"; an "economic mission," "to operate the Company on a sound financial basis...increasing value for our shareholders and creating career opportunities and financial rewards for our employees"; and a "social mission," "to operate the Company in a way that actively recognizes the central role that business plays in the structure of society by initiating innovative ways to improve the quality of life of a broad community: local, national and international." This statement has been further simplified by the Company's statement of "Leading with Progressive Values Across our Business." "Underlying the mission of Ben & Jerry's is the determination to seek new and creative ways of addressing all three parts, while holding a deep respect for individuals inside and outside the Company and for the communities of which they are a part." Since 1988, the Company's Annual Report to Stockholders has contained a "social report" on the Company's performance during the year. The Company's social mission has always been about more than philanthropy, product donations and community relations. Ben & Jerry's has strived to integrate into its day-to-day business decisions a concern for the community and to seek ways to lead with its progressive values.

The Company makes cash contributions equal to 7.5% of its pretax profits to philanthropy through The Ben & Jerry's Foundation (the "Foundation"), Community Action Teams, which are employee led groups from each of its five Vermont sites, and through corporate grants. Excluded from the 7.5% are contributions out of a portion of the proceeds of incidental operations, not directly relating to Ben & Jerry's core business of the manufacturing and selling of Ben & Jerry's frozen desserts, such as a portion of the admission fees for plant tours. Also excluded from the 7.5% are corporate sponsorships that have as one of their purposes the furtherance of Ben & Jerry's marketing goals. For 1999, the 7.5% amounted to approximately $1,120,000. The amount of the Company's cash contribution is subject to review by the Board of Directors from time to time in light of the Company's cash needs, its operating results, existing conditions in the industry and other factors deemed relevant by the Board. See "The Ben & Jerry's Foundation."

In some instances where the Company pays royalties for the licensed use of a flavor name, the licensor donates all or a portion of these royalties to charitable organizations. For example, in 1997, the Company launched Phish Food(TM) ice cream and during 1999 paid the Vermont-based band Phish $244,918 in royalties. The band established the Water Wheel Foundation to support the protection and preservation of Lake Champlain.

Ben & Jerry's maintains a special tie to the Vermont community in which it has its origins. The Company donates product to public events and community celebrations in the Vermont area. As already noted, Community Action Teams at each site make grants in Vermont. Also, the Company, acting as an agent, transfers funds to charitable organizations throughout Vermont derived from the sale of product to participating Vermont retail grocers.

Ben & Jerry's has, through the years, taken actions intended to strengthen the Company's ability to remain an independent Vermont-based company focused on carrying out its three-part corporate mission. Ben & Jerry's believes these actions have been in the best interests of the Company, its stockholders, employees, suppliers, customers and the Vermont community. See "Anti-Takeover Effects of Class B Common Stock, Class A Preferred Stock, Classified Board of Directors, Vermont Legislation and Shareholders' Rights Plans."

In 1991, the Company decided to pay not less than a certain minimum price for its dairy ingredients other than yogurt cultures, to bring the price up to an amount based upon the average price for dairy products in certain prior periods. This commitment is part of an effort to foster the supply of Vermont dairy products and thereby also seek to maintain the long-term viability of the Company's source of dairy ingredients, against the marketplace background of a continuing trend of decreasing family dairy farms in Vermont.

In early 1994, the Company's agreement with the St. Albans Cooperative Creamery was amended to include, as a condition for payment of the premium, an assurance from the St. Albans Cooperative Creamery that the milk and cream purchased by the Company will not come from cows that have been treated with recombinant Bovine Growth Hormone ("rBGH"), a synthetic growth hormone approved by the FDA.

In December 1997, the St. Albans Cooperative Creamery's board of directors approved a motion to allow for controlled use of rBGH by a limited number of member farms beginning July 1, 1998. The Co-op assures that it will continue to provide Ben & Jerry's with rBGH-free dairy supply. The Company pays a premium to the Co-op for member farms that do not use rBGH.

In 1992, the Company became a signatory to the CERES Principles adopted by the Community for Environmentally Responsible Economies. The CERES Principles established an environmental ethic with criteria by which investors and others can assess the environmental performance of companies. Ben & Jerry's is also a member of Business for Social Responsibility, Inc. ("BSR"), an organization in San Francisco, California, which promotes a concept of business profitability that includes environmental responsibility and social equity. Ben & Jerry's is also a member of the Social Venture Network and Vermont Businesses for Social Responsibility.

The Super Premium Ice Cream, Frozen Yogurt and Sorbet Market

The packaged ice cream industry includes economy, regular, premium, premium plus and super premium products. Super premium ice cream is generally characterized by a greater richness and density than other kinds of ice cream. This higher quality ice cream generally costs more than other kinds and is usually marketed by emphasizing quality, flavor selection, texture and brand image. Other types of ice cream are largely marketed on the basis of price.

Super Premium Ice Cream, Super Premium Frozen Yogurt And, More Recently, super premium sorbet have become an important part of the frozen dessert industry. In response to the demand for lower fat, lower cholesterol products, the Company introduced its own super premium low fat frozen yogurt in 1992. In February 1996, the Company introduced lactose-free and cholesterol-free sorbet. In 1997, Ben & Jerry's introduced a new line of low fat ice cream. In 1999 the Company introduced 14 new flavors and 3 new novelty products.

Based on information provided by Information Resources, Inc., a software and marketing information services company ("IRI"), the Company believes that total annual U.S. sales in supermarkets at retail prices (defined as grocery stores with annual revenues of at least $2 million) of super premium and premium plus ice cream, frozen yogurt and sorbet were approximately $572 million in 1999 compared with about $518 million in 1998. All of the information in this paragraph is taken from IRI data.

Ben & Jerry's Super Premium Ice Cream, Frozen Yogurt and Sorbet

Ben & Jerry's ice cream has a high level of butterfat and low level of air incorporation ("overrun") during the freezing process. The approximate fat content is 15% (excluding add-ins). The approximate overrun is 20%. These physical attributes give the ice cream the rich taste and dense, creamy texture that characterizes super premium ice creams. The fat content of the ice cream is derived primarily from the butterfat in the cream, and secondarily from egg yolks. The ice cream mix consists of cream, beet sugar, non-fat milk solids, egg yolks and natural stabilizers.

Ben & Jerry's frozen yogurt is a high quality frozen yogurt with approximately 2% fat (excluding add-ins) and approximately 30% overrun. The fat content of frozen yogurt comes from the cream used in the base mix. All our frozen yogurt products are sweetened with beet sugar and corn syrup. The Company uses cultured yogurt in the manufacturing of our frozen yogurt dessert products, purchased from yogurt manufacturers who use Vermont dairy ingredients.

Ben & Jerry's fruit sorbets are fat free frozen desserts with an overrun of approximately 20%. The chocolate sorbet is a low fat product with approximately 2% fat (from cocoa and chocolate liquor). All sorbets are sweetened with beet sugar and corn syrup. The water used to manufacture sorbet is Vermont Pure(TM) Spring Water.

In 1997 and 1998, Ben & Jerry's introduced a line of low fat ice cream flavors. These low fat ice creams offer high quality, all natural ingredients with less than three grams of fat and 40% overrun. The product line offers exciting flavor combinations, chunks of candy, and swirls of variegates with extraordinary flavor.

All Ben & Jerry's frozen desserts are made of the finest quality ingredients. Its ingredients contain no preservatives or artificial components (except the flavoring component in one of the candies that the Company purchases). To date, the Company has not experienced any difficulty in obtaining the dairy products used to make its frozen desserts. The various flavorings, add-ins and variegates are readily available from multiple suppliers throughout the country.

All the Company's plants include mix-batching facilities, which allows Ben & Jerry's to manufacture its own dessert mixes. Ben & Jerry's designed and modified special machinery to mix large chunks of cookies, candies, fruits and nuts into our frozen desserts. The Company has also designed proprietary processes for swirling variegates (dessert sauces) into its finished products.

The Company also makes ice cream novelty products, including a variety of ice cream bars such as Cherry Garcia(R), Cookie Dough, Phish Stick(TM), Dilbert's World(TM)-Totally Nuts(TM) and S'mores(TM) Bars.

Ben & Jerry's other license agreements include licenses from the estate of Jerry Garcia, formerly of the Grateful Dead rock group, with respect to the Company's Cherry Garcia(R) flavor; political cartoonist Garry Trudeau and Andrews McMeel Universal with respect to the Company's Doonesberry(R) flavor of the sorbet line of products; Wavy Gravy for the flavor Wavy Gravy; with Phish Merchandising, Inc. with respect to Phish Food(TM) and Phish Stick(TM), a flavor launched in February of 1997; and from United Feature Syndicate, Inc. for use of the trademark Dilbert for the flavor Dilbert's World(TM)-Totally Nuts(TM) introduced in 1998.

Manufacturing

The Company manufactures Ben & Jerry's super premium ice cream and frozen yogurt pints at its Waterbury, Vermont, plant. The Company's Springfield, Vermont, plant is used for the production of ice cream novelties, ice cream, frozen yogurt, low fat ice cream and sorbet packaged in bulk, pints, quarts and half gallons. The Company manufactures Ben & Jerry's super premium ice cream, frozen yogurt, frozen smoothies and sorbet in packaged pints, 12 oz. and single serve containers at its St. Albans, Vermont plant. The Company generally operates its plants two shifts a day, five to seven days per week, depending upon demand requirements.

On October 19, 1999, the Company announced a plan to shift manufacturing of its frozen novelty line of business from a company-owned plant in Springfield, Vermont, to third party co-packers to improve the Company's competitive position, gross margins and profitability. This action resulted in the write-off of assets associated with the ice cream novelty business, asset impairment charges of other manufacturing assets and costs associated with severance for those employees who do not accept the Company's offer of relocation. The implementation of this manufacturing restructuring program resulted in a pre-tax special charge to earnings of approximately $8.6 million in the fourth quarter of 1999 that was primarily non-cash. This plan will be executed during 2000 and is expected to result in improving the Company's profitability during the year 2000. Outsourcing its novelty business will enable the Company to introduce a wider range of novelty products in future periods.

Markets and Customers

The Company markets packaged pints, quarts, 1/2 gallons, single-serve containers and novelty products primarily through supermarkets, other grocery stores, convenience stores and other retail food outlets. The Company markets ice cream, frozen yogurt and sorbet in 2 1/2-gallon bulk containers primarily through franchised (and Company-owned) Ben & Jerry's scoop shops, through restaurants and food service accounts (i.e. stadiums, airports, cafeterias, hotels, etc.).

Ben & Jerry's products are distributed through independent ice cream distributors; with some exceptions, only one distributor is appointed for each territory for supermarkets. In most areas, sub-distributors are used to distribute to the smaller classes of trade. Company trucks and other distributors distribute products that are sold in Vermont and upstate New York.

In late August 1998 - January 1999, Ben & Jerry's redesigned its distribution network to create more Company control over sales and more efficiency in the distribution of its products. Under the redesign, Ben & Jerry's increased direct sales calls by its own sales force (as distinguished from calls by the distributors' sales forces) to all grocery and chain convenience stores and has a network where no distributor of Ben & Jerry's products has a majority percentage of the Company's distribution. Under the distribution network redesign which commenced in April-May 1999 and was fully effective September 1, 1999, Ice Cream Partners, a joint venture of the U.S. ice cream operations of Nestle and The Pillsbury Company ("Pillsbury") distributes Ben & Jerry's products in specified territories; the balance of domestic deliveries are distributed primarily by Dreyer's Grand Ice Cream, Inc. ("Dreyer's"), with Dreyer's handling a smaller volume (than before) of Ben & Jerry's distribution in other specified territories, and in part by other independent regional distributors, most of whom are already acting as distributors for Ben & Jerry's. Under the redesign, no single distributor is expected to handle over 40% of Ben & Jerry's distribution, as compared with Dreyer's distribution activities accounting for approximately 57% of the Company's net sales in 1998 and 1997.

Pursuant to the distribution network redesign, Ben & Jerry's entered into an agreement with Pillsbury which, as amended in January 1999, provides for distribution of Ben & Jerry's products on a non-exclusive basis in various areas of the United States beginning September 1, 1999, and in certain areas commencing April - May 1999. This agreement was assigned to Ice Cream Partners (a joint venture between Pillsbury and Nestle formed in October 1999), by the Company and was amended in December 1999. The agreement with Ice Cream Partners may not be terminated `(except for cause) by Ice Cream Partners or Ben & Jerry's until an effective date in the year 2003. The agreement further provides that Ben & Jerry's may earlier terminate without cause by making certain specified payments (except that such payments are not required under specified circumstances) and it contains additional provisions relating to any termination upon a change in control of either party. The use of sub-distributors by Ice Cream Partners is limited under the Agreement.

In January 1999, the Company concluded a new distribution agreement, also on a non-exclusive basis, with Dreyer's, effective for distribution which commenced September 1, 1999. This agreement pertains to a smaller geographic area than that which was covered under the prior distribution agreement and is on terms and conditions different in some respects from those applicable under the prior distribution agreement. The terms as to the prices received by the Company from Dreyer's purchases of the Company's ice cream products are in line with the new Agreement the Company entered into with Pillsbury and assigned to Ice Cream Partners, and are more favorable to the Company than in the past.

The new agreement with Dreyer's may be terminated by either party on not less than six months' notice except that no such notice may be given during the months of October - March in any year. The prior agreement had given Dreyer's certain territorial exclusivity, limited the sale by Dreyer's of competitive products (Dreyer's brands and certain brands of other ice cream competitors), and had contained provisions for payment by the terminated party in the event of a change in control of the terminated party.

While the Company believes that its relationships with Dreyer's and its other distributors generally have been satisfactory and that these relationships have been instrumental in the Company's growth, the Company has, at times, experienced difficulties in maintaining these relationships to its satisfaction. The Company believes that the distribution network redesign in August 1998 - 1999 gave it more control over the Company's distribution. However, due to the consolidations in the distribution arena, including the combination of the Nestle and Pillsbury domestic ice cream operations into Ice Cream Partners, available distribution alternatives are limited. Accordingly, there can be no assurance that such difficulties with distributors, which may be related to actions by the Company's distributors (which include, as the Company's two principal distributors, its two principal competitors in the marketplace, will not have a material adverse effect on the Company's business. Loss of one or more of the Company's principal distributors or termination of one or more of the related distribution agreements or certain action by the production/marketing units of these two principal distributors could have a material adverse effect on the Company's business.

Marketing

Ben & Jerry's marketing is characterized by a strategic discipline that continues to build brand equity, a solid reputation for the Company and, most importantly, profitable customer relationships.

Ben & Jerry's marketing strategies remain consistent with the Company's three-part mission. Building on Ben & Jerry's significant brand name recognition, the Company continues to emphasize the high quality, natural ingredients in its products while highlighting its commitment to social change through innovative promotional and advertising campaigns. Ben & Jerry's continues to facilitate brand awareness by focusing its marketing efforts on communicating the Company's unique business approaches via Public Relations campaigns designed to generate unpaid newspaper, magazine, radio and TV news coverage. Company founders Ben Cohen and Jerry Greenfield continue to make personal appearances on TV and radio.

A 1999 Harris Interactive Poll regarding public perceptions of corporate reputability ranked Ben & Jerry's fifth overall, and first in the "social responsibility" category. The survey, the results of which were published in the Wall Street Journal, used an assessment tool developed at New York University's Stern School of Business to measure a company's reputation, based upon several key areas - social responsibility, emotional appeal, products and services.

In 1999, Ben & Jerry's became the first U.S. ice cream company to convert a significant portion of its pint containers to a more environmentally-friendly unbleached paperboard. The debut of the Company's "Eco-Pint" made headlines in consumer and financial press nationwide.

Additional media opportunities in 1999 included placement of the Company's products in popular sitcoms and movies. Scenes from an upcoming feature film starring Jim Carrey were filmed at the Company's Waterbury factory. Ben & Jerry's conducts guided tours of its facility in Waterbury, Vermont to approximately 300,000 visitors annually, making it the single most popular tourist attraction in the state.

Ben & Jerry's increased internet presence was driven by several web-based promotions, including a Halloween promotion in which consumers were invited to trick or treat online, and a Yahoo!(R) Careers promotion in which consumers could win a day as a Ben & Jerry's flavor developer.

Ben & Jerry's scoop shops, substantially all of which are franchised, also contributed significantly to the growth of the brand. In April, Ben & Jerry's marked its 21st Anniversary with a record-breaking Free Cone Day covered by local and national media. Almost 200 Ben & Jerry's scoop shops served up more than a half million free cones as a "thank you" to their customers in this coast-to-coast event.

Franchise Program

As of December 25, 1999, there were 164 North American Franchise and Satellite scoop shops compared to 147 as of December 26, 1998. In addition to our traditional Franchise and Satellite locations, the Company has 8 PartnerShop(R) Franchises, 19 Featuring Franchises and 12 Scoop Station Franchises.

Ben & Jerry's Franchise Scoop Shops sell Ben & Jerry's ice cream, frozen yogurt, sorbet, private label hot fudge, baked goods and toppings. The menu items also include coffee, beverages, fruit smoothies, ice cream cakes, novelties and gift items.

A PartnerShop(R) Franchise is a scoop shop that is awarded to a not-for-profit organization. PartnerShop(R) franchises are arrangements that permit not-for-profit organizations to own franchised scoop shops that serve as an employment resource and potentially a source of revenue for the not-for-profit groups. The Company waives the normal franchisee fee of $30,000. In addition the Company provides expertise in the start-up and operation of the PartnerShop(R).

A Featuring Franchise is a business that has a scoop shop within its location, much like a store within a store. Featuring Franchises are often located in airports, stadiums, college campuses and similar venues.

In the beginning of 1999, the Company began offering another franchise concept, a Scoop Station franchise. As of December 25, 1999, there were 12 Scoop Station franchises. These franchises are located within businesses; generally a smaller product line is served from a pre-fabricated unit.

At year-end, there were nine company-owned scoop shops: four in Vermont, two in Las Vegas, Nevada and three locations in Paris, France. Internationally, there are nine Ben & Jerry's franchised scoop shops in Israel; four in Canada, three in the Netherlands, one in Lebanon and one in Peru.

New scoop shops are opened under existing Development Agreements and under new Single Store Agreements. Development Agreements require a franchisee to develop a particular number of units annually according to the terms of their Agreement. The Company has assorted franchise concepts that include traditional shops in a variety of settings, five PartnerShop(R) Featuring Franchises and Scoop Station Franchises. Franchise Agreements generally have initial terms of five to ten years and renewal terms. The Scoop Station is a limited concept with a smaller menu offering; the initial term is generally two years.

International

The Company regularly investigates the possibilities of entering new markets. Ben & Jerry's ice cream products are now distributed internationally in the United Kingdom and Israel and are available in parts of Japan, Ireland, France, Canada, the Netherlands, Belgium, Singapore, Peru and Lebanon.

In May 1998, the Company signed a non-exclusive licensing agreement with Delicious Alternative Desserts, LTD, to manufacture, sell and distribute Ben & Jerry's products through the wholesale distribution channels in Canada for royalty payments based upon a percentage of the licensee's sales. This agreement is for a five-year period with a renewal option. In connection with this agreement, the Company received 4,000,000 Common Shares of Delicious Alternative Desserts, LTD which represents less than 5% of total issued outstanding common shares on a fully diluted basis, and the right to designate one director.

In 1987, the Company granted an exclusive license to manufacture and sell Ben & Jerry's ice cream in Israel. Effective February 26, 1999, the Company acquired a 60% ownership interest in its Israeli licensee, The American Company for Ice Cream Manufacturing E.I. Ltd, for $1 million. The acquisition was accounted for using the purchase method of accounting and, accordingly, the costs of the acquisition have been allocated to assets acquired. The excess of the acquisition costs over the fair values of the net assets and liabilities acquired was $1.7 million and has been recorded as goodwill, which is being amortized on a straight-line basis over 15 years.

In 1997, the Company signed an Importation and Marketing Agreement with one of the largest food retailers in Japan for sale through Japanese retail stores of Ben & Jerry's products manufactured in Vermont in a special size. Following a test market, the product was launched in 1998. In March 1999, the Company established a wholly-owned subsidiary in Japan for purposes of importing, marketing and selling its products in Japan. Beginning in January 2000, the Company imports all products into the Japan market through an agreement with a Japanese trading company.

Competition

The super premium ice cream, frozen yogurt and sorbet business is highly competitive, with the distinction between the super premium category and the "adjoining" premium and premium plus categories less marked than in the past. The Company's two principal competitors are The Haagen-Dazs operation of Ice Cream Partners and Dreyer's/Edys, which introduced its Dreamery(TM) super premium line in the fall of 1999. Other significant frozen dessert competitors are Columbo, Healthy Choice and Starbucks (distributed by Dreyer's). Haagen-Dazs has a significant share of the markets that the Company has entered in recent years. Haagen-Dazs has also entered substantially more foreign markets than the Company (including certain markets in Europe and the Pacific Rim). Haagen-Dazs and certain other competitors also market flavors using pieces of cookies and candies as ingredients. As part of Ben & Jerry's distribution network redesign, the Pillsbury U.S. ice cream operations (now part of the Ice Cream Partners Joint Venture) became a principal distributor for the Company's products.

In January and September 1999, Dreyer's launched two lines of super-premium ice cream, Godiva and Dreamery(TM), with significant marketing programs including radio, outdoor and television advertising as well as heavy price discounting to gain trial. The Godiva and Dreamery(TM) products are marketed primarily in pints. Additional super premium products may be introduced by other ice cream competition.

In the ice cream novelty segment, the Company competes with several well-known brands, including Haagen-Dazs and Dove Bars, manufactured by a division of Mars, Inc., Good Humor (owned by Unilever), Nestle products and many private label brands. All of these other brands have achieved far larger shares of the novelty market than the Company.

During 1999, the premium category again experienced increased promotional activity driven by the national competition between Dreyer's Grand Ice Cream, Inc., a principal distributor for the Company, and Breyer's Ice Cream (owned by Unilever, a large international food company). In accordance with Dreyer's strategic plan to accelerate the sales of their branded premium products Dreyer's has increased its consumer marketing efforts and continued expansion of its distribution system into additional U.S. markets. There are a number of other super premium brands, including some regional ice cream companies and some new entries. Increased competition and the increased consumer demand for a variety of frozen dessert products, combined with limited shelf space within supermarkets, may have made market entry harder and has already forced some brands out of some markets. The ability to introduce innovative new flavors on a periodic basis is also a significant competitive factor. The Company expects strong competition to increase, including price/promotional competition and competition for adequate distribution and limited shelf space within the frozen dessert category in supermarkets and other food retail outlets.

Seasonality

The ice cream, frozen yogurt and frozen dessert industry generally experiences the highest volume during the spring and summer months and the lowest volume in the winter months.

Regulation

The Company is subject to regulation by various governmental agencies, including the United States Food and Drug Administration and the Vermont Department of Agriculture. It must also obtain licenses from certain states where Ben & Jerry's products are sold. The criteria for labeling low fat/low cholesterol and other health-oriented foods was revised in 1994 and in some respects was made more stringent by the FDA. The Company, like other companies in the food industry, made changes in its labeling in response to these regulations and is in compliance. The Company cannot predict the impact of possible further changes that it may be required to make in response to legislation, rules or inquiries made from time to time by governmental agencies. FDA regulations may, in certain instances, affect the ability of the Company, as well as others in the frozen desserts industry, to develop and market new products. Nevertheless, the Company does not believe these legislative and administrative rules and regulations will have a significant impact on its operations.

In connection with the operation of all its plants, the Company must comply with the Federal and Vermont environmental laws and regulations relating to air quality, waste management and other related land use matters. The Company maintains wastewater discharge permits for all of its manufacturing locations. All the plants pre-treat production effluent prior to discharge to the municipal treatment facility. The Company believes that it is in compliance with all of the required operational permits relating to environmental regulations.

Trademarks

The marks Ben & Jerry's, Ben & Jerry's Portrait, Ben & Jerry's Ice Cream on A First Name Basis, Chubby Hubby, Chunky Monkey, Coffee, Coffee BuzzBuzzBuzz!, Cool Britannia, Dastardly Mash, Hunka Hunka Burnin' Fudge, Lids for Kids, More Chunks Less Bunk, New York Super Fudge Chunk, One World One Heart, PartnerShop,

Peace Pop, Rainforest Chunk, Today's Euphoric Flavors, Totally Nuts, Vanilla Like It Oughta' Be, Vermont's Finest and World's Best are registered trademarks of the Company.

Cherry Garcia(R), Phish Food(R), Phish Stick(R), Wavy Gravy(TM), Doonesberry(R), Heath(R) and Dilbert's World(R) are Ben & Jerry's proprietary flavor names and are licensed to the Company.

Employees

At December 25, 1999, Ben & Jerry's employed 841 people including full-time, part-time and temporary employees. This represents a 12% increase from the 751 people employed by the Company at December 26, 1998.

During 1998, a union organizing effort took place at the Company's St. Albans, Vermont, plant within the Maintenance Department. By a majority vote all full-time and regular part-time maintenance team members employed by the Company agreed to be represented by the International Brotherhood of Electrical Workers (IBEW). The Company signed an agreement in November 1999, with the Union. As of December 25, 1999, 16 employees were members of IBEW.

The Ben & Jerry's Foundation

In 1985, Ben Cohen, co-founder of the Company, contributed a portion of the equity of the Company which he then owned to The Ben & Jerry's Foundation, Inc., a charitable organization under Section 501(c)(3) of the Internal Revenue Code, in order to enable the Foundation to sell such equity in 1985 and invest the net proceeds (approximately $598,000) in income-producing securities to generate funds for future charitable grants. The Foundation, with its employee-led grant-making committee under supervision of the Foundation's directors, provides the principal means for carrying out the Company's charitable cash giving policy across the nation. The Foundation continues to target its grants to small grassroots social change organizations.

In October 1985, pursuant to stockholder authorization, the Company issued to the Foundation all of the 900 authorized shares of Class A Preferred Stock. The Class A Preferred Stock gives the Foundation a special class voting right to act with respect to certain mergers and other Business Combinations (as defined in the Company's charter). The issuance of Preferred Stock was designed to perpetuate the relationship between the Foundation and the Company and to assist the Company in its determination to remain an independent business headquartered in Vermont.

Anti-Takeover Effects of Class B Common Stock, Class A Preferred Stock, Classified Board of Directors, Vermont Legislation and Shareholder Rights Plans.

The holders of Class A Common Stock are entitled to one vote for each share held on all matters voted on by stockholders, including the election of directors. The holders of Class B Common Stock are entitled to ten votes for each share held in the election of directors and on all other matters. The Class B Common Stock is generally nontransferable as such, and there is no trading market for the Class B Common Stock. The Class B Common Stock is freely convertible into Class A Common Stock on a share-for-share basis and transferable thereafter. A stockholder who does not wish to complete the prior conversion process may effect a sale by simply delivering the certificate for such shares of Class B Common Stock to a broker, properly endorsed. The broker may then present the certificate to the Company's transfer agent which, if the transfer is otherwise in good order, will issue to the purchaser a certificate for the number of shares of Class A Common Stock thereby sold.

The Company has been advised that Mr. Jerry Greenfield (Chairperson and a director of the Company), Mr. Ben Cohen (Vice-Chairperson and a director of the Company) and Mr. Jeff Furman (a director and formerly a consultant to the

Company) (collectively, the "Principal Stockholders") presently intend to retain substantial numbers of shares of Class B Common Stock. As a result of conversions by "public" stockholders of Class B Common Stock, in order to enable their sales of such securities, the Class B Common Stock is now held disproportionately by Company insiders, including the above-named three directors who are Principal Stockholders. See "Security Ownership of Certain Beneficial Owners and Management." As of February 25, 2000, these three principal individual stockholders held shares representing 47% of the aggregate voting power in elections of directors and various other matters and 17% of the aggregate common equity outstanding, permitting them, as a practical matter, generally to decide elections of directors and various other questions submitted to a vote of the Company's stockholders even though they might sell substantial portions of their Class A Common Stock.

The Board of Directors, without further stockholder approval, may issue additional authorized but unissued shares of Class B Common Stock in the future and sell shares of Class B Common Stock held in the Company's treasury. In 1985, Ben Cohen, one of the Company's co-founders, contributed a portion of the equity in the Company, which he then owned, to the Ben & Jerry's Foundation, Inc. Two of the three current directors of the Foundation, Messrs. Greenfield and Furman, are also directors of the Company. The Class A Preferred Stock gives the Foundation a class voting right to act with respect to certain Business Combinations (as defined in the Company's charter). The 1985 issuance of the Class A Preferred Stock to the Foundation effectively limits the voting rights that holders of the Class A Common Stock and Class B Common Stock, the owners of virtually all of the equity in the Company, would otherwise have with respect to Business Combinations (as defined). This may have the effect of limiting such common stockholders participation in certain transactions such as mergers, other

Business Combinations (as defined) and tender offers, whether or not such transactions might be favored by such common stockholders.

At the 1997 Annual Meeting the shareholders approved amendments to the Company's Articles of Association to (a) classify the Board into three classes, as nearly equal as possible, so that each director (after a transitional period) will serve for three years, with one class of directors being elected each year; (b) provide that directors may be removed only for cause and with the approval of at least two-thirds of the votes cast on the matter by all of the outstanding shares of capital stock of the Company entitled to vote generally in the election of directors; (c) provide that any vacancy resulting from such a removal may be filled by two-thirds of the directors then in office; and (d) increase the stockholder vote required to alter, amend, repeal or adopt any provision inconsistent with these amendments approved by stockholders in 1997 to at least two-thirds of the votes cast on the matter by all of the outstanding shares of capital stock of the Company entitled to vote generally in the elections of directors, voting together.

Also, in April 1998, the Legislature of the State of Vermont amended a provision of the Vermont Business Corporation Act to provide that the directors of a Vermont corporation may also consider, in determining whether an acquisition offer or other matter is in the best interests of the corporation, the interests of the corporation's employees, suppliers, creditors and customers, the economy of the state in which the corporation is located and including the possibility that the best interests of the corporation may be served by the continued independence of the corporation. Also, in August 1998, following approval by its Board of Directors, the Company put in place two Shareholder Rights Plans, one pertaining to the Class A Common Stock and one pertaining to the Class B Common Stock. These Plans are intended to protect stockholders by compelling someone seeking to acquire the Company to negotiate with the Company's Board of Directors in order to protect stockholders from unfair takeover tactics and to assist in the maximization of stockholder value. These Rights Plans, which are common for public companies in the United States, may also be deemed to be "anti-takeover" provisions in that the Board of Directors believes that these Plans will make it difficult for a third party to acquire control of the Company on terms which are unfair or unfavorable to the stockholders.

The Class B Common Stock, which may be converted into shares of Class A Common Stock by a specified vote of the Board, the Class A Preferred Stock, which may be redeemed by a specified vote of the Board, the Classified Board of Directors and the Shareholder Rights Plans may be deemed to be "anti-takeover" provisions in that the Board of Directors believes the existence of these securities and the 1997 amendments to the Articles of Association will make it difficult for a third party to acquire control of the Company on terms opposed by the holders of the Class B Common Stock, including primarily the Principal Stockholders and the Foundation, or for incumbent management and the Board of Directors to be removed. See also "Risk Factors" in Item 7 of this Report.

The Company believes that these provisions of the Articles of Association, the amendment to the Vermont Business Corporation Act and the Shareholder Rights Plans, reduce the possibility that a third party could effect a change, including a tender offer or a sudden or surprise change in the composition of the Company's Board of Directors, without the support of the incumbent Board and, accordingly, that adoption of these items strengthened Ben & Jerry's ability to remain an independent, Vermont-based company focused on carrying out its three-part corporate mission, which Ben & Jerry's believes is in the best interest of the Company, its stockholders, employees, suppliers, customers and the Vermont community.

Indications of Interest to Acquire the Company; Alternative Transactions

The Company announced on December 2, 1999 that it had received Indications of Interest to acquire the Company at prices significantly above the closing price on NASDAQ on the day before the December 2, 1999 press release ($21.00). These Indications of Interest are subject to conditions and, together with Alternative Transactions under which the Company would remain an independent company, are being considered by the Board of Directors.

The Company's policy, as regularly disclosed in its filings with the Securities and Exchange Commission, has been to remain an independent Vermont-based company focused on its three-part corporate mission, emphasizing product quality, economic reward and a commitment to the community, contributing 7 1/2% of its profit before tax to charities, including donations to The Ben & Jerry's Foundation, Inc.

No decision has been made by the Board with respect to any of these indications of interest or as to any sale of the Company or Alternative Transactions under which the Company would remain independent ("Alternative Transactions") (See "Risk Factors Indications of Interest: to Acquire the Company; Alternative Transactions"), and no implications should be drawn from this Report as to what definitive decision will be reached by the Board after it has concluded its deliberations or as to the timing of any decision.

        * * *

ITEM 3.   LEGAL PROCEEDINGS

The Company is subject to certain litigation and claims in the ordinary course of business which management believes are not material to the Company's business.

        * * *

ITEM 5.   MARKET FOR REGISTRANT'S COMMON EQUITY AND RELATED STOCKHOLDER MATTERS

The Company's Class A Common Stock is traded on the NASDAQ National Market System under the symbol BJICA. The following table sets forth for the period December 28, 1997 through February 25, 2000, the high and low closing sales prices of the Company's Class A Common Stock for the periods indicated.

	High	Low
1998		
First Quarter	$ 19	$ 14
Second Quarter	21 1/8	17
Third Quarter	19 7/8	13 1/16
Fourth Quarter	23 7/8	14 7/8
1999		
First Quarter	$ 27	$ 21 3/8
Second Quarter	30	24 3/8
Third Quarter	29	17 7/8
Fourth Quarter	28 1/4	15 13/16
2000		
First Quarter through February 25, 2000	$ 29 1/4	$ 21 1/4

The Class B Common Stock is generally non-transferable and there is no trading market for the Class B Common Stock. However, the Class B Common Stock is freely convertible into Class A Common Stock on a share-for-share basis, and transferable thereafter. A stockholder who does not wish to complete the prior conversion process may effect a sale by simply delivering the certificate for such shares of Class B Stock to a broker, properly endorsed. The broker may then present the certificate to the Company's transfer agent which, if the transfer is otherwise in good order, will issue to the purchaser a certificate for the number of shares of Class A Common Stock thereby sold.

As of February 25, 2000 there were 9,979 holders of record of the Company's Class A Common Stock and 1,922 holders of record of the Company's Class B Common Stock.

* * *

ITEM 6.   SELECTED FINANCIAL DATA

The following table contains selected financial information for the Company's fiscal years 1995 through 1999.

Summary of Operations (In thousands except per share data)

	Fiscal Year				
	1999	1998	1997	1996	1995
Net sales	$237,043	$209,203	$174,206	$167,155	$155,333
Cost of sales	145,291	136,225	114,284	115,212	109,125
Gross profit	91,752	72,978	59,922	51,943	46,208
Selling, general & administrative expenses	78,623	63,895	53,520	45,531	36,362
Special charge1	8,602	--	--	--	--
Other income (expense) - net	681	693	(118)	(77)	(441)
Income before income taxes	5,208	9,776	6,284	6,335	9,405
Income taxes	1,823	3,534	2,388	2,409	3,457
Net income	$ 3,385	$ 6,242	$ 3,896	$ 3,926	$ 5,948
Net income per share - diluted	$0.46	$0.84	$0.53	$0.54	$0.82
Shares outstanding - diluted	7,405	7,463	7,334	7,230	7,222

Balance Sheet Data:

	Fiscal Year				
	1999	1998	1997	1996	1995
Working capital	$ 42,805	$ 48,381	$ 51,412	$ 50,055	$ 51,023
Total assets	150,602	149,501	146,471	136,665	131,074
Long-term debt and capital lease obligations	16,669	20,491	25,676	31,087	31,977
Stockholders' equity2	89,391	90,908	86,919	82,685	78,531

1. In 1999 the Company finalized a plan to shift manufacturing of its frozen novelty line of business from a Company-owned plant in Springfield, Vermont to third party co-packers to improve the Company's competitive position, gross margin and profitability. This action resulted in fourth quarter 1999 write-off of assets associated with the ice cream novelty and other manufacturing assets and costs associated with severance for those employees who do not accept the Company's offer of relocation.

2. No cash dividends have been declared or paid by the Company on its capital stock since the Company's organization. The Company intends to reinvest earnings for use in its business and to finance future growth. Accordingly, the Board of Directors does not anticipate declaring any cash dividends in the foreseeable future.

ITEM 7. MANAGEMENT'S DISCUSSION AND ANALYSIS OF FINANCIAL CONDITION AND RESULTS
        OF OPERATIONS

Results of Operations

The following table shows certain items as a percentage of net sales, which are
included in the Company's Statement of Income.

	Percentage of Net Sales Fiscal Year			Annual Increase (Decrease)		
	1999	1998	1997	1999 Compared To 1998	1998 Compared To 1997	1997 Compared To 1996
Net sales	100.0%	100.0%	100.0%	13.3%	20.1%	4.2%
Cost of sales	61.3	65.1	65.6	6.7	19.2	(0.8)
Gross profit	38.7	34.9	34.4	25.7	21.8	15.4
Selling, general and administrative expense	33.2	30.5	30.7	23.0	19.4	17.5
Special charge	3.6	--	--	--	--	--
Other income (expense)	0.3	0.3	(0.1)	0.2	687.3	53.2
Income before income taxes	2.2	4.7	3.6	(46.7)	55.6	(0.8)
Income taxes	0.8	1.7	1.4	(48.4)	8.0	(0.9)
Net income	1.4%	3.0%	2.2%	(45.8)%	60.2%	(0.8)%

Net Sales

Net sales in 1999 increased 13.3% to $237 million from $209 million in 1998
primarily due to growth in the U.S. marketplace as well as the United Kingdom.
Total worldwide pint volume increased 8.9% compared to 1998, which was primarily
attributable to the Company's original line of products. This volume increase
was combined with a price increase of 3.3% on pints sold to U.S. distributors
that went into effect in July 1998. Total worldwide unit volume of 2 1/2 gallon
bulk container products increased 16.7% compared to the same period in 1998.

Packaged sales (primarily pints) represented 83% of total net sales in 1999, 81%
of total net sales in 1998 and 84% of total net sales in 1997. Net sales of 2
1/2 gallon bulk containers represented approximately 9% of total net sales in
1999 and 8% of total net sales in 1998 and 1997. Net sales of novelty products
(including single servings) accounted for approximately 6% of total net sales in
1999, 9% of total net sales in 1998 and 6% of total net sales in 1997. This
decrease is due to a decline in sales of single serve containers to the Japanese
market in comparison to the prior year. Net sales from the Company's retail
stores represented 2% of total net sales in 1999, 1998 and 1997.

International sales were $25.3, $17.4, and $7.6 million in 1999, 1998 and 1997,
respectively, which represents 11% of total net sales in 1999, 8% in 1998 and 4%
in 1997. The increase in 1999 was primarily due to increased sales in the United
Kingdom partially offset by a decrease in net sales to the Japanese market.

Net sales in 1998 increased 20.1% to $209 million from $174 million in 1997.
Total worldwide pint volume increased 10% compared to 1997 which was primarily
attributable to the Company's original line of products. This volume increase
was combined with a price increase of 3% on pints sold to distributors that went
into effect in July 1998. Total worldwide unit volume of 2 1/2 gallon bulk
container products increased 17% compared to the same period in 1997.

Cost of Sales

Cost of sales in 1999 increased approximately $9 million or 6.7% over the same
period in 1998 and overall gross profit as a percentage of net sales increased
from 34.9% in 1998 to 38.7% in 1999. The higher gross profit as a percentage of
net sales resulted from decreased dairy commodity costs, a 3.3% distributor
price increase effective in July 1998 and a price increase in connection with

the Company's distribution redesign in 1999, better plant utilization due to higher production volumes and improved efficiencies in the plants.

Cost of sales in 1998 increased approximately $22 million or 19% over the same period in 1997 and overall gross profit as a percentage of net sales increased from 34.4% in 1997 to 34.9% in 1998. The slightly higher gross profit as a percentage of net sales resulted from increases in selling prices effective in January 1998 and July 1998, better plant utilization due to higher production volumes and a decrease in reserves for potential product obsolescence, partially offset by substantial increases in dairy commodity costs. In response to higher dairy costs the Company instituted a 3% price increase effective in July 1998 for its packaged pint products and a combined 10% price increase for its 2 1/2 gallon bulk containers effective in January 1998 and July 1998 to offset these increased costs. See Risk Factors, "Volatile Cost of Raw Materials."

Selling, General and Administrative Expenses

Selling, general and administrative expenses increased 23.0% to $78.6 million in 1999 from $63.9 million in 1998 and increased as a percentage of net sales to 33.2% in 1999 from 30.5% in 1998. The $14.7 million dollar increase primarily reflects increased selling expenses related to the Company's earlier restructuring of its distribution system and increased advertising and promotions expenses. In addition the Company is investing more heavily in its international operations, most notably in the United Kingdom, Japan and Israel in order to capitalize on further opportunities to grow its ice cream sales outside the United States. Selling, general and administrative expenses also reflect increased salaries, recruiting and training expenses related to building more infrastructure to manage its business, and in the fourth quarter of 1999 higher expenses for professional advisors, including its investment bankers, consultants and legal counsel, related to the Company's review and consideration of the Indications of Interest to Acquire the Company and Alternative Transactions.

Selling, general and administrative expenses increased 19% to $64 million in 1998 from $54 million in 1997 and decreased slightly as a percentage of net sales to 30.5% in 1998 from 30.7% in 1997. The $10 million increase in expenses is attributable to increased sales and marketing expenses to support the launch of a new line of premium plus ice cream under the name of Newman's Own(TM) All Natural Ice Cream, increased international costs, increases in radio advertising, in-store programs to drive product trial and brand awareness, scoop truck marketing and the rollout of the new pint package design.

Special Charge

Following a comprehensive review of its manufacturing operations, the Company finalized a plan to shift manufacturing of its frozen novelty line of business from a company-owned plant in Springfield, Vermont to third party co-packers to improve the Company's competitive position, gross margin and profitability. This action resulted in a fourth quarter 1999 non-recurring pre-tax charge of $8.6 million ($.78 per common share, after tax) consisting of the write-off of assets associated with the ice cream novelty and other manufacturing assets and costs associated with severance for those employees who do not accept the Company's offer of relocation. This plan to shift novelty manufacturing will be executed during

2000. The outsourcing of its ice cream novelty business will enable the Company to introduce a wider range of novelty products in the future and increase its flexibility.

Other Income (Expense)

Interest income decreased to $1.9 million in 1999 compared to $2.2 million in 1998. This decrease in interest income was due to a lower average invested balance throughout the period. Interest expense decreased $254,000 compared to 1998. This decrease is due to the $5 million Senior Notes principal payment made in September 1999 partially offset by increased interest expense for debt acquired through the Company's 60% ownership interest in its Israeli licensee.

Interest income increased from $1.9 million in 1997 to $2.2 million in 1998. The increase in interest income was due to higher average invested balance throughout 1998. Interest expense in 1998 decreased $104,000 in 1998 as compared to 1997 due to the $5 million Senior Notes principal installment payment. Other income (expense) increased in 1998 from other expense of $118,000 in 1997 to other income of $693,000 in 1998. This is primarily due to increased losses associated with foreign currency exchange in comparison to 1997, combined with income received from the Company's cost basis investment.

Income Taxes

The Company's effective income tax rate in 1999 decreased to 35% from 36% in 1998 and 38% in 1997. The decrease was a result of lower state income taxes, more tax-exempt interest income, and the overall geographic mix of earnings. Management expects 2000's effective income tax rate to remain at approximately 35% based upon the expected geographic mix of earnings.

Net Income

Net income for 1999, excluding the non-recurring special charge discussed above, increased to $9.0 million from $6.2 million in 1998. Diluted net income per share excluding the non-recurring special charge was $1.21 in 1999 compared to $0.84 in 1998. Net income after reflecting the special charge was $3.4 million in 1999. Net income as a percentage of net sales was 3.8% (excluding the non-recurring special charge) and 1.4% (after reflecting the special charge) in 1999 as compared to 3.0% in 1998 and 2.2% in 1997.

During the fourth quarter of 1999 and continuing into the first quarter of 2000, the Company incurred significant expenditures (classified within S,G&A) for services of its investment banker, consultants and legal counsel, including separate legal counsel for various directors, in connection with the investigations and deliberations of the Board with respect to the various Indications of Interest to acquire the Company and Alternative Transactions under consideration by the Board. These expenditures are expected to continue until the Board makes a definitive decision on this subject.

The Company expects to face increased domestic competition in the Year 2000, which will require increased selling and marketing expenditures, and may result in a slower rate of growth in net sales and may well have an adverse effect on future results, as compared with results for the Year 1999. See "Risk Factors" generally.

Seasonality

The Company typically experiences more demand for its products during the summer than during the winter.

Inflation

Inflation has not had a material effect on the Company's business to date, with the exception of dairy raw material commodity costs. See the Risk Factors below. Management believes that the effects of inflation and changing prices were successfully managed in 1999, with both margins and earnings being protected through a combination of pricing adjustments, cost control programs and productivity gains.

Liquidity and Capital Resources

As of December 25, 1999 the Company had $46.6 million of cash, cash equivalents and short term investments ($25.3 million of cash and cash equivalents and $21.3 million of marketable securities), a $638,000 decrease since December 26, 1998. Net cash provided by operations in 1999 was $20.3 million. Uses of cash included increases in accounts receivable and inventories of $7.5 million and $405,000 respectively, $5.3 million to pay down debt and capital lease obligations, repurchase of company stock of $7.2 million, and additions to property, plant and equipment, primarily for equipment upgrades at the Company's manufacturing facilities, of $8.8 million. The increase in accounts receivable is due to a contractual change in the Company's distribution agreement with Dreyer's Grand Ice Cream effective in January 1999, which altered the payment terms from 14 to 28 days. Partially offsetting these uses of cash was an increase in accounts payable and accrued expenses of $7 million. The increase in accounts payable and accrued expenses reflects additional liabilities related to both the Japanese and Israeli operations.

In addition the Company acquired a 60% interest in its Israeli licensee for $1 million in February, 1999. Cash acquired in the transaction was $858,000. In June 1999, the Company acquired the assets of one of its franchisees, which included Las Vegas, Nevada territory rights and two scoop shops, for approximately $870,000 net of cash acquired.

In September 1999, the Company completed its previously announced repurchase program commenced in September 1998, which authorized the Company to purchase shares of the Company's Class A Common Stock up to an aggregate cost of $5 million for use for general corporate purposes. In September 1999 the Board of Directors approved an additional $3 million for stock repurchases of its Class A common shares. During the year ended December 25, 1999 the Company repurchased a total of 364,100 shares of the Company's Class A Common Stock for approximately $7.2 million.

The Company's short and long-term debt at December 25, 1999 includes $20 million aggregate principal amount of Senior Notes issued in 1993 and 1994. The second principal payment of $5 million was paid in October 1999 and the remainder of principal is payable in annual installments through 2003.

The Company anticipates capital expenditures in 2000 of approximately $9.0 million. Most of these projected capital expenditures relate to equipment upgrades and enhancements at the Company's manufacturing facilities, computer-related expenditures and build out of Company-owned scoop shops.

The Company has available two $10,000,000 unsecured working capital line of credit agreements with two banks. Interest on borrowings under the agreements is set at the banks' base rate or at LIBOR plus a margin based on a pre-determined formula. No amounts were borrowed under these or any bank agreements during 1999. The working capital line of credit agreements expire December 23, 2001.

Management believes that internally generated funds, cash, cash equivalents and marketable securities and equipment lease financing and/or borrowings under the Company's two unsecured bank lines of credit will be adequate to meet anticipated operating and capital requirements.

Impact of Year 2000

The Company experienced no significant disruptions in mission critical information technology and non-information technology systems and believes those systems successfully responded to the Year 2000 date change. The Company expensed approximately $620,000 during 1999 in connection with remediating its systems. The Company is not aware of any material problems resulting from Year 2000 issues, either with its products, its internal systems, or the products and services of third parties. The Company will continue to monitor its mission critical computer applications and those of its suppliers and vendors throughout the year 2000 to ensure that any latent Year 2000 matters that may arise are addressed promptly.

Euro Conversion

On January 1, 1999 certain member countries of the European union established fixed conversion rates between their existing currencies and the European Union's common currency ("the euro"). The former currencies of the participating countries are scheduled to remain legal tender as denominations of the euro until January 1, 2002 when the euro will be adopted as the sole legal currency.

The Company has evaluated the potential impact on its business, including the ability of its information systems to handle euro-denominated transactions and the impact on exchange costs and currency exchange rate risks. The conversion to the euro is not expected to have a material impact on the Company's operations or financial position.

Forward-Looking Statements

This section, as well as other portions of this document, includes certain forward-looking statements about the Company's business, new products, sales, dairy ingredient commodity costs, other expenditures and cost savings, effective tax rate, operating and capital requirements and financing. Any such statements are subject to risks that could cause the actual results or needs to vary materially and are also subject to changes in connection with any potential Indications of Interest to acquire the Company or Alternative Transactions. These risks are discussed below.

In addition, forward-looking statements may be included in various other Company documents to be issued in the future and in various oral statements by Company representatives to security analysts and investors from time to time.

Risk Factors

Dependence on Independent Ice Cream Distributors. Historically, the Company has been dependent on maintaining satisfactory relationships with Dreyer's Grand Ice Cream, Inc. ("Dreyer's") and the other independent ice cream distributors that have acted as the Company's exclusive or master distributor in their assigned territories. In 1998, Dreyer's distributed significantly more than a majority of the sales of Ben & Jerry's products. While the Company believes its relationships with Dreyer's and its other distributors generally have been satisfactory and have been instrumental in the Company's growth, the Company has at times experienced difficulty in maintaining such relationships to its satisfaction. In August 1998 - January 1999, the Company redesigned its distribution network, entering into a distribution agreement with The Pillsbury Company ("Pillsbury") and a new agreement with Dreyer's. These arrangements took

effect in September 1999, except for certain territories which were effective in April - May 1999. The Company believes the terms of the new arrangements will be more favorable to the Company and expects that, under the distribution network redesign, no one distributor will account for more than 40% of the Company's net sales. The October 1999 transfer of the Haagen-Dazs unit to the recently formed Pillsbury/Nestle ice cream joint venture has presented certain opportunities/difficulties for the Company, which entered into an amendment with the Ice Cream Partners joint venture in December 1999, in connection with the assignment of that agreement from Pillsbury to the joint venture.

However, both the recently formed Pillsbury/Nestle ice cream joint venture (through its Haagen-Dazs super premium ice cream unit), and Dreyer's with its fall 1999 super premium ice cream market entry are direct competitors of the Company.

Since available distribution alternatives are limited and continue to be adversely impacted by consolidation in the industry, there can be no assurance that difficulties in maintaining satisfactory relationships with its two principal distributors (who are competitors) and its other distributors, some of which are also competitors of the Company, will not have a material adverse effect on the Company's business (See "Business - Markets and Customers").

Growth in Sales and Earnings. In 1999, net sales of the Company increased 13.3% to $237 million from $209 million in 1998. Total worldwide pint volume increased 8.9% compared to 1998. Based on information provided by Information Resources, Inc., a software and marketing information services company ("IRI"), the Company believes that the U.S. super premium and premium plus ice cream, frozen yogurt and sorbet industry category sales increased 10% in 1999 compared to 1998. Given these overall domestic super premium industry trends, the successful introduction of innovative flavors on a periodic basis has become increasingly important to sales growth by the Company. Accordingly, the future degree of market acceptance of any of the Company's new products, which will be accompanied by significant promotional expenditures, is likely to have an important impact on the Company's 2000 and future financial results. However, the Company expects that, due to increased domestic competition, it will need to increase its selling and marketing expenses and that its rate of growth in net sales may be slower in the current Year 2000, which may be expected to adversely affect earnings (See "Management's Discussion and Analysis of Financial Conditions and Results of Operations").

Competitive Environment. The super premium frozen dessert market is highly competitive, with the distinctions between the super premium category and the "adjoining" premium and premium plus categories less marked than in the past. As noted above, the ability to successfully introduce innovative flavors on a periodic basis that are accepted by the marketplace is a significant competitive factor. In addition, the Company's principal competitors, two of which are distributors for the Company, are large companies with resources significantly greater than the Company's. In January and September 1999 Dreyer's launched two lines of super premium ice cream, Godiva and Dreamery(TM), with significant marketing programs including radio, outdoor and television advertising as well as heavy price discounting to gain trial. The Godiva and Dreamery(TM) products are marketed primarily in pints. Additional super premium products may be introduced by other ice cream competitors. In October 1999, the U.S. ice cream operations of Pillsbury (Haagen-Dazs) and Nestle were consolidated into a joint venture, Ice Cream Partners. See "Business Competition" and "Business: The Super Premium Frozen Dessert Market." The Company expects strong competition to continue and increase, including competition for the limited shelf space for the frozen dessert category in supermarkets and other retail food outlets, the impact of consolidation in the retail food outlets and increased competition from the Company's two principal distributors.

Volatile Cost of Raw Materials. Management believes that the general trend of volatility in dairy ingredient commodity costs may continue. While dairy commodity costs for 1999, and especially for the second half of 1999, were lower than in 1998, it is possible that at some future date both gross margins and earnings may not be adequately protected by pricing adjustments, cost control programs and productivity gains.

Reliance on a Limited Number of Key Personnel. The success of the Company is significantly dependent on the services of Perry Odak, the Chief Executive Officer, and a limited number of executive managers working under Mr. Odak, as well as certain continued services of Jerry Greenfield, the Chairperson of the

Board and co-founder of the Company, and Ben Cohen, Vice Chairperson and co-founder of the Company. Loss of the services of any of these persons could have a material adverse effect on the Company's business. See "Directors and Executive Officers of the Company."

The Company's Social Mission. The Company's basic business philosophy is embodied in a three-part "mission statement," which includes a "social mission" to "operate the Company in a way that actively recognizes the central role that business plays in the structure of society by initiating innovative ways to improve the quality of life of a broad community: local, national and international. Underlying the mission of Ben & Jerry's is the determination to seek new and creative ways of addressing all three parts, while holding a deep respect for individuals inside and outside the Company and for the communities of which they are a part." The Company believes that implementation of its social mission, which is integrated into the Company's business, has been beneficial to the Company's overall financial performance. However, it is possible that at some future date the amount of the Company's energies and resources devoted to its social mission could have some material adverse financial effect. See "Business-Introduction" and "Business-Marketing."

International. Total international net sales represented approximately 11% of total consolidated net sales in 1999. The Company's principal competitors have substantial market shares in various countries outside the United States, principally Europe and Japan. The Company sells product in the United Kingdom and France, through license arrangements in the Netherlands and Belgium. Sales were also made in Japan andSingapore and the Company started selling in Peru and Lebanon in 1999 under license arrangements. In 1987, the Company granted an exclusive license to manufacture and sell Ben & Jerry's products in Israel. In 1999, the Company made an investment of $1 million in its Israeli licensee, which gave the Company a 60% ownership interest. In May 1998, the Company signed a Licensing Agreement with Delicious Alternative Desserts, LTD to manufacture, sell and distribute Ben & Jerry's products through the wholesale distribution channels in Canada. The Company is investigating the possibility of further international expansion. However, there can be no assurance that the Company will be successful in all of its present international markets or in entering (directly, or indirectly through licensing) on a long-term profitable basis, such additional international markets as it selects.

Control of the Company. The Company has two classes of common stock - the Class A Common Stock, entitled to one vote per share, and the Class B Common Stock (authorized in 1987), entitled, except to the extent otherwise provided by law, to ten votes per share. Ben Cohen, Jerry Greenfield and Jeffrey Furman (collectively the "Principal Stockholders") hold shares representing 47% of the aggregate voting power in elections for directors, permitting them as a practical matter to elect all members of the Board of Directors and thereby effectively control the business, policies and management of the Company. Because of their significant holdings of Class B Common Stock, the Principal Stockholders may continue to exercise this control even if they sell substantial portions of their Class A Common Stock. See "Security Ownership of Certain Beneficial Owners and Management."

In addition, the Company issued all of the authorized Class A Preferred Stock to the Foundation in 1985. The Class A Preferred Stock gives the Foundation a class voting right to act with respect to certain Business Combinations (as defined in the Company's charter) and significantly limits the voting rights that holders of the Class A Common Stock and Class B Common Stock, the owners of virtually all of the equity in the Company, would otherwise have with respect to such Business Combinations. See "Business The Ben & Jerry's Foundation."

Also, in April 1998, the Legislature of the State of Vermont amended a provision of the Vermont Business Corporation Act to provide that the directors of a

Vermont corporation may also consider, in determining whether an acquisition offer or other matter is in the best interests of the corporation, the interests of the corporation's employees, suppliers, creditors and customers, the economy of the state in which the corporation is located and including the possibility that the best interests of the corporation may be served by the continued independence of the corporation. Also, in August 1998, following approval by its Board of Directors, the Company put in place two Shareholder Rights Plans, one pertaining to the Class A Common Stock and one pertaining to the Class B Common Stock. These Plans are intended to protect stockholders by compelling someone seeking to acquire the Company to negotiate with the Company's Board of Directors in order to protect stockholders from unfair takeover tactics and to assist in the maximization of stockholder value. These Rights Plans, which are common for public companies in the United States, may also be deemed to be "anti-takeover" provisions in that the Board of Directors believes that these Plans will make it difficult for a third party to acquire control of the Company on terms which are unfair or unfavorable to the stockholders.

While the Board of Directors believes that the Class B Common Stock and the Class A Preferred Stock are important elements in keeping Ben & Jerry's an independent, Vermont-based business focused on its three-part corporate mission, the Class B Common Stock and the Class A Preferred Stock (which may be converted into Class A Common Stock or redeemed in the case of the Class A Preferred Stock, as the case may be, by the specified votes of the Board of Directors) may be deemed to be "anti-takeover" provisions in that the Board of Directors believes the existence of these securities will make it difficult for a third party to acquire control of the Company on terms opposed by the holders of the Class B Common Stock, including primarily the Principal Stockholders, or The Foundation, or for incumbent management and the Board of Directors to be removed.

In addition, the 1997 amendments to the Company's Articles of Association to classify the Board of Directors and to add certain other related provisions and the April 1998 Vermont Legislative Amendment of the Vermont Business Corporation Act and the Shareholder Rights Plans put in place in August, 1998 (see "Anti-Takeover Effects of Class B Common Stock, Class A Common Stock, Class A Preferred Stock, Classified Board of Directors, Vermont Legislation and Shareholder Rights Plans" in Item 1) may be deemed to be "anti-takeover" provisions in that the Board of Directors believes that these amendments and legislation will make it difficult for a third party to acquire control of the Company on terms opposed by the holders of the Class B Common Stock, including primarily the Principal Stockholders and the Foundation, or for incumbent management and the Board of Directors to be removed.

Indications of Interest to Acquire the Company; Alternative Transactions. The Company announced on December 2, 1999 that it had received indications of interest to acquire the Company and Alternative Transactions to acquire the Company at prices significantly above the closing price on NASDAQ on the day before the December 2, 1999 press release ($21.00). These Indications of Interest are subject to conditions and, together with Alternative Transactions under which the Company would remain an independent company, are being considered by the Board of Directors.

The Company's policy, as regularly disclosed in its filings with the Securities and Exchange Commission, has been to be an independent Vermont-based company focused on its three-part corporate mission, emphasizing product quality, economic reward and a commitment to the community, contributing 7 1/2% of its profit before tax to charities, including donations to The Ben & Jerry's Foundation, Inc.

No decision has been made by the Board with respect to any of these Indications of Interest or as to any sale of the Company or as to any Alternative

Transaction under which the Company would remain an independent company, and no implications should be drawn from this Report as to what definitive decision will be reached by the Board after it has concluded its deliberations or as to the timing of any decision. As noted under "Management's Discussion and Analysis of Financial Condition and Results of Operations," the Board has been receiving advice from its investment banker, consultants hired in connection with this matter and counsel, including separate counsel hired by various individual directors. The matters relating to the Indications of Interest or Alternative Transactions present a different set of risks and opportunities for the Company and its continued independence, which could materially affect the future operations and results of the Company.

            * * *

[ITEM 8. FINANCIAL STATEMENTS]

            * * *

ANNUAL REPORT ON FORM 10-K

LIST OF FINANCIAL STATEMENTS

YEAR ENDED DECEMBER 25, 1999

BEN & JERRY'S HOMEMADE, INC.

SOUTH BURLINGTON, VERMONT

INDEX TO CONSOLIDATED FINANCIAL STATEMENTS

REPORT OF ERNST & YOUNG LLP
INDEPENDENT AUDITORS

The Board of Directors and Stockholders
Ben & Jerry's Homemade, Inc.

We have audited the accompanying consolidated balance sheets of Ben & Jerry's Homemade, Inc. as of December 25, 1999 and December 26, 1998, and the related consolidated statements of income, stockholders' equity, and cash flows for each of the three years in the period ended December 25, 1999. Our audits also included the financial statement schedule listed in the Index at Item 14(a)(2). These financial statements and schedule are the responsibility of the Company's management. Our responsibility is to express an opinion on these financial statements and schedule based on our audits.

We conducted our audits in accordance with auditing standards generally accepted in the United States. Those standards require that we plan and perform the audit to obtain reasonable assurance about whether the financial statements are free of material misstatement. An audit includes examining, on a test basis, evidence supporting the amounts and disclosures in the financial statements. An audit also includes assessing the accounting principles used and significant estimates made by management, as well as evaluating the overall financial statement presentation. We believe that our audits provide a reasonable basis for our opinion.

In our opinion, the consolidated financial statements referred to above present fairly, in all material respects, the consolidated financial position of Ben & Jerry's Homemade, Inc. at December 25, 1999 and December 26, 1998 and the consolidated results of its operations and its cash flows for each of the three years in the period ended December 25, 1999, in conformity with accounting principles generally accepted in the United States. Also, in our opinion, the related financial statement schedule, when considered in relation to the basic financial statements taken as a whole, presents fairly in all material respects the information set forth therein.

/s/ERNST & YOUNG LLP

Boston, Massachusetts
January 21, 2000

BEN & JERRY'S HOMEMADE, INC.
CONSOLIDATED BALANCE SHEETS
(In thousands except per share amounts)

	December 25, 1999	December 26, 1998
ASSETS		
Current assets:		
Cash and cash equivalents	$ 25,260	$ 25,111
Short-term investments	21,331	22,118
Trade accounts receivable (less allowance of $966 in 1999 and $979 in 1998 for doubtful accounts)	18,833	11,338
Inventories	13,937	13,090
Deferred income taxes	5,609	7,547
Prepaid expenses and other current assets	2,377	3,105
Total current assets	87,347	82,309
Property, plant and equipment, net	56,557	63,451
Investments	200	303
Deferred income taxes	656	
Other assets	5,842	3,438
	$ 150,602	$ 149,501
LIABILITIES & STOCKHOLDERS' EQUITY		
Current liabilities:		
Accounts payable and accrued expenses	$ 38,915	$ 28,662
Current portion of long-term debt and obligations under capital leases	5,627	5,266
Total current liabilities	44,542	33,928
Long-term debt and obligations under capital leases	16,669	20,491
Deferred income taxes		4,174
Stockholders' equity:		
$1.20 noncumulative Class A preferred stock - par value $1.00 per share, redeemable at $12.00 per share; 900 shares authorized, issued and outstanding; aggregated preference on liquidation - $9,000	1	1
Class A common stock - $.033 par value; authorized 20,000,000 shares; issued: 6,759,276 at December 25, 1999 and 6,592,392 at December 26, 1998	223	218
Class B common stock - $.033 par value; authorized 3,000,000 shares; issued: 801,813 at December 25, 1999 and 824,480 at December 26, 1998	27	27
Additional paid-in-capital	52,961	50,556
Retained earnings	48,713	45,328
Accumulated other comprehensive loss	(460)	(151)
Treasury stock, at cost: 644,606 Class A and 1,092 Class B shares at December 25, 1999 and 291,032 Class A and 1,092 Class B shares at December 26, 1998	(12,074)	(5,071)
Total stockholders' equity	89,391	90,908
	$ 150,602	$ 149,501

See notes to consolidated financial statements.

BEN & JERRY'S HOMEMADE, INC.
CONSOLIDATED STATEMENTS OF INCOME
(In thousands except per share amounts)

	Fiscal Year Ended		
	December 25, 1999	December 26, 1998	December 27, 1997
Net sales	$ 237,043	$ 209,203	$ 174,206
Cost of sales	145,291	136,225	114,284
Gross profit	91,752	72,978	59,922
Selling, general and administrative expenses	78,623	63,895	53,520
Special charge	8,602		
Other income (expense):			
Interest income	1,924	2,248	1,938
Interest expense	(1,634)	(1,888)	(1,992)
Other income (expense), net	391	333	(64)
	681	693	(118)
Income before income taxes	5,208	9,776	6,284
Income taxes	1,823	3,534	2,388
Net income	$ 3,385	$ 6,242	$ 3,896
Shares used to compute net income per common share			
Basic	7,077	7,197	7,247
Diluted	7,405	7,463	7,334
Net income per common share			
Basic	$ 0.48	$ 0.87	$ 0.54
Diluted	$ 0.46	$ 0.84	$ 0.53

See notes to consolidated financial statements.

Consolidated Statements of Stockholders' Equity
(In thousands except share data)

	Preferred Stock Par Value	Common Stock Class A Par Value	Common Stock Class B Par Value	Additional Paid-in Capital	Retained Earnings	Accumulated Other Comprehensive Loss
Balance at December 28, 1996	$1	$210	$29	$48,753	$35,190	$(118)
Net income					3,896	
Common stock issued under stock purchase plan (15,406 Class A shares)		1		148		
Conversion of Class B shares to Class A shares (31,451 shares)		1				
Common stock issued under stock and option plans (83,267 Class A shares)		2		907		
Repurchase of common stock (77,500 Class A shares)						
Issuance of treasury stock for compensation (20,000 Class A shares)				(127)		
Foreign currency translation adjustment						(11)
Net comprehensive income						
Balance at December 27, 1997	1	214	29	49,681	39,086	(129)
Net income					6,242	
Common stock issued under stock purchase plan (14,277 Class A shares)				179		
Conversion of Class B shares to Class A shares (41,755 shares)		2	(2)			
Common stock issued under stock and option plans (41,525 Class A shares)		2		696		
Repurchase of Treasury Stock (166,500 Class A shares)						
Foreign currency translation adjustment						(22)
Net comprehensive income						
Balance at December 26, 1998	1	218	27	50,556	45,328	(151)
Net Income					3,385	
Common stock issued under stock purchase plan (9,995 Class A shares)				175		
Conversion of Class B shares to Class A shares (22,667 shares)						
Common stock issued under stock and option plans (134,222 Class A shares)		5		2,164		
Repurchase of common stock (364,100 Class A shares)						
Issuance of treasury stock contributed to 401(K) Savings Plan (10,526 Class A Shares)				66		
Foreign currency translation adjustment						15
Unrealized losses on available for sale securities						(324)
Net comprehensive income						
Balance at December 25, 1999	$1	$223	$27	$52,961	$48,713	$(460)

[Continued on following page.]

[Continued from previous page.]

	Treasury Stock		Total Stockholders' Equity	Comprehensive Income
	Class A Cost	Class B Cost		
Balance at December 28, 1996	$(1,375)	$(5)	$82,685	
Net income			3,896	$3,896
Common stock issued under stock purchase plan (15,406 Class A shares)			149	
Conversion of Class B shares to Class A shares (31,451 shares)			1	
Common stock issued under stock and option plans (83,267 Class A shares)			909	
Repurchase of common stock (77,500 Class A shares)	(988)		(988)	
Issuance of treasury stock for compensation (20,000 Class A shares)	405		278	
Foreign currency translation adjustment			(11)	(11)
Net comprehensive income				$3,885
Balance at December 27, 1997	(1,958)	(5)	86,919	
Net income			6,242	$6,242
Common stock issued under stock purchase plan (14,277 Class A shares)			179	
Conversion of Class B shares to Class A shares (41,755 shares)				
Common stock issued under stock and option plans (41,525 Class A shares)			698	
Repurchase of Treasury Stock (166,500 Class A shares)	(3,108)		(3,108)	
Foreign currency translation adjustment			(22)	(22)
Net comprehensive income				$6,220
Balance at December 26, 1998	(5,066)	(5)	90,908	
Net Income			3,385	$3,385
Common stock issued under stock purchase plan (9,995 Class A shares)			175	
Conversion of Class B shares to Class A shares (22,667 shares)				
Common stock issued under stock and option plans (134,222 Class A shares)			2,169	
Repurchase of common stock (364,100 Class shares)	(7,187)		(7,187)	
Issuance of treasury stock contributed to 401(K) Savings Plan(10,526 Class A shares)	184		250	
Foreign currency translation adjustment			15	15
Unrealized losses on available for sale securities			(324)	(324)
Net comprehensive income				$3,076
Balance at December 25, 1999	$(12,069)	$(5)	$89,391	

See notes to consolidated financial statements.

BEN & JERRY'S HOMEMADE, INC.
CONSOLIDATED STATEMENTS OF CASH FLOWS
(In thousands)

| | Fiscal Year Ended | | |
	December 25, 1999	December 26, 1998	December 27, 1997
Cash flows from operating activities:			
Net income	$ 3,385	$ 6,242	$ 3,896
Adjustments to reconcile net income to net cash provided by operating activities:			
Depreciation and amortization	9,202	8,181	7,711
Provision for bad debts	349	50	630
Deferred income taxes	(2,674)	(2,510)	(1,599)
Stock compensation	250		405
Special charge	8,602		
Loss on disposition of assets	76	112	124
Changes in operating assets and liabilities:			
Accounts receivable	(7,926)	1,460	(5,318)
Inventories	(405)	(1,968)	4,243
Prepaid expenses	(121)	(501)	(64)
Accounts payable and accrued expenses	6,810	5,385	5,868
Income taxes payable(receivable)	2,756	(364)	1,743
Net cash provided by operating activities	20,304	16,087	17,639
Cash flows from investing activities:			
Additions to property, plant and equipment	(8,825)	(8,770)	(5,236)
Proceeds from sale of assets	48		48
Changes in other assets	(764)	(1,082)	(425)
Decrease (increase) in investments	566	(20,879)	(76)
Acquisitions, net of cash acquired	(1,012)		
Net cash used for investing activities	(9,987)	(30,731)	(5,689)
Cash flows from financing activities:			
Repayments of long-term debt and capital leases	(5,328)	(5,321)	(669)
Repurchase of common stock	(7,187)	(3,108)	(988)
Proceeds from issuance of common stock	2,343	877	932
Net cash used for financing activities	(10,172)	(7,552)	(725)
Effect of exchange rate changes on cash	4	(11)	(11)
Increase (decrease) in cash and cash equivalents	149	(22,207)	11,214
Cash and cash equivalents at beginning of year	25,111	47,318	36,104
Cash and cash equivalents at end of year	$ 25,260	$ 25,111	$ 47,318

See notes to consolidated financial statements.

Notes to Consolidated Financial Statements
Dollars in tables in thousands except share data

1.   SIGNIFICANT ACCOUNTING POLICIES

Business

Ben & Jerry's Homemade, Inc. (the "Company") makes and sells super premium ice cream and other frozen dessert products through distributors and directly to retail outlets primarily located in the United States and selected foreign countries, including Company-owned and franchised ice cream parlors.

Principles of Consolidation

The consolidated financial statements include the accounts of the Company and all its majority owned subsidiaries. Intercompany accounts and transactions have been eliminated.

Fiscal Year

The Company's fiscal year is the 52 or 53 weeks ending on the last Saturday in December. Fiscal years 1999, 1998 and 1997 consisted of the 52 weeks ended December 25, 1999, December 26, 1998 and December 27, 1997, respectively.

Use of Estimates

The preparation of the financial statements in accordance with accounting principles generally accepted in the United States requires management to make estimates and assumptions that affect the amounts reported in the financial statements and accompanying notes. Actual results could differ from those estimates.

Inventories

Inventories are stated at the lower of cost or market. Cost is determined by the first-in, first-out method.

Cash Equivalents

Cash equivalents represent highly liquid investments with maturities of three months or less at date of purchase.

Investments

Management determines the appropriate classification of investments at the time of purchase and reevaluates such designation as of each balance sheet date. At December 25, 1999 and December 26, 1998, the Company considers all its investments, except for certificates of deposit, as available for sale. Available-for-sale securities are carried at fair value, with the unrealized gains and losses reported as a separate component of stockholders' equity. Held-to-maturity securities are stated at amortized cost, adjusted for amortization of premium and accretion of discounts to maturity. Such amortization is included in interest income. Realized gains and losses and declines in value judged to be other-than-temporary on available-for-sale securities are included in income. The cost of securities sold is based on the specific identification method. Interest and dividends on investments are included in interest income.

Notes to Consolidated Financial Statements
Dollars in tables in thousands except share data

Concentration of Credit Risk

Financial instruments, which potentially subject the Company to significant concentration of credit risk, consist of cash and cash equivalents, investments and trade accounts receivable. The Company places its investments in highly rated financial institutions, obligations of the United States Government and investment grade short-term instruments. No more than 20% of the total investment portfolio is invested in any one issuer or guarantor other than United States Government instruments which limits the amount of credit exposure.

The Company sells its products primarily to well-established frozen dessert distribution or retailing companies throughout the United States and in certain foreign countries. The Company performs ongoing credit evaluations of its customers and maintains reserves for potential credit losses. Historically, the Company has not experienced significant losses related to investments or trade receivables.

Property, Plant and Equipment

Property, plant and equipment are carried at cost. Depreciation, including amortization of leasehold improvements, is computed using the straight-line method over the estimated useful lives of the related assets. Amortization of assets under capital leases is computed on the straight-line method over the lease term and is included in depreciation expense.

Other Assets

Other assets include intangible and other noncurrent assets. Intangible assets are reviewed for impairment based on an assessment of future operations to ensure that they are appropriately valued. Intangible assets are amortized on a straight-line basis over their estimated economic lives.

Translation of Foreign Currencies

Assets and liabilities of the Company's foreign operations are translated into United States dollars at exchange rates in effect on the balance sheet date. Income and expense items are translated at average exchange rates prevailing during the year. Translation adjustments are included in accumulated other comprehensive income. Transaction gains or losses are recognized as other income or expense in the period incurred. Translation and transaction gains or losses have been immaterial for all periods presented.

Foreign Currency Hedging

The Company hedges foreign currency risk by entering into future options based on projected forecasts of a portion of the Company's foreign operations. In addition, from time to time, the Company enters into forward contracts to hedge foreign currency denominated sales. Realized and unrealized gains or losses on contracts or options that hedge anticipated cash flows are determined by comparison of contract or option value upon execution (realized) and at each balance sheet for open contracts or options (unrealized). Realized gains and losses are recognized at the balance sheet date as other income or expense for the period. In the case of options entered into based on projected forecasts, unrealized gains and losses are recognized upon the determination that circumstances have changed which cause the hedged instrument to be speculative in nature.

Notes to Consolidated Financial Statements
Dollars in tables in thousands except share data

Transaction gains or losses have been immaterial for all periods presented.

Revenue Recognition

The Company recognizes revenue and the related costs when product is shipped. The Company recognizes franchise fees as income for individual stores when services required by the franchise agreement have been substantially performed and the store opens for business. Franchise fees relating to area franchise agreements are recognized in proportion to the number of stores for which the required services have been substantially performed. Franchise fees recognized as income and included in net sales were approximately $520,000, $708,000 and $553,000 in 1999, 1998 and 1997, respectively.

Advertising

Advertising costs are expensed as incurred. Advertising expense (excluding cooperative advertising with distribution companies) amounted to approximately $17.5 million, $10.6 million and $6.7 million in 1999, 1998 and 1997, respectively.

Income Taxes

The Company accounts for income taxes under the liability method. Under the liability method, deferred tax liabilities and assets are recognized for the tax consequences of temporary differences between the financial reporting and tax bases of assets and liabilities.

Stock Based Compensation

The Company's stock option plans provide for the grant of options to purchase shares of the Company's common stock to both employees and consultants. The Company has elected to follow Accounting Principles Board Opinion No. 25, Accounting for Stock Issued to Employees (APB 25) and related interpretations and provides pro forma disclosures of the compensation expense determined under the fair value provisions of Finanical Accounting Standards Board Statement No. 123 (FAS 123), Accounting for Stock-Based Compensation. In accounting for its employee stock options under APB 25, when the exercise price of the Company's employee stock options equals the market price of the underlying stock on the date of grant, no compensation expense is recognized. No compensation expense was recognized for any of the years presented. The Company has followed FAS 123 for stock options granted to non-employees as required.

Earnings Per Share

Effective December 28, 1997, the Company adopted Statement No. 128, Earnings per Share. Basic earnings per share have been computed based on the weighted-average number of common shares outstanding during the period. Diluted earnings per share have been computed based upon the weighted-average number of common shares outstanding during the year, adjusted for the dilutive effect of shares issuable upon the exercise of stock options and warrants determined based upon the average market price for the period.

Comprehensive Income

As of December 28, 1997, the Company adopted Statement No. 130, Reporting Comprehensive Income (FAS 130). FAS 130 establishes new rules for the reporting and display of comprehensive income and its components; however, the adoption of this statement had no impact on the Company's net income or shareholders' equity. Statement 130 requires unrealized gains or losses on the Company's available-for-sale securities and foreign currency translation adjustments to be included in other comprehensive income.

Notes to Consolidated Financial Statements
Dollars in tables in thousands except share data

Segment Information

As of December 28, 1997, the Company adopted Statement No. 131, Disclosures about Segments of an Enterprise and Related Information (FAS 131). FAS 131 superseded Statement No. 14, Financial Reporting for Segments of a Business Enterprise. FAS 131 establishes standards for the way that public business enterprises report information about operating segments in annual financial statements and requires that those enterprises report selected information about operating segments in interim financial reports. FAS 131 also establishes standards for related disclosures about products and services, geographic areas and major customers. The adoption of FAS 131 did not affect results of operations or financial position, but did affect the disclosure of segment information. See Note 17.

Impact of Recently Issued Accounting Standards

In June 1998, the Financial Accounting Standards Board issued Statement of Financial Accounting Standards No. 133, "Accounting for Derivative Instruments and Hedging Activities" ("FAS 133"). Statement 133 will require the Company to record all derivatives on the balance sheet at fair value. For derivatives that are hedges, changes in the fair value of derivatives will be offset by changes in the underlying hedged item in earnings in the same period. In June 1999, the Financial Accounting Standards Board delayed the effective date of FAS 133 to the first quarter of fiscal years beginning after June 15, 2000. The Company expects to adopt FAS 133 in the First quarter of fiscal year 2001.

2. BUSINESS ACQUISITIONS

Effective February 26, 1999, the Company acquired a 60% interest in its Israeli licensee for $1 million. The acquisition was accounted for under the purchase method, and the results of operations of the acquired business have been included in the consolidated financial statements since the date of acquisition. The purchase price was allocated based on estimated fair values at the date of acquisition. The excess of the acquisition costs over the fair values of the net assets and liabilities acquired was $1.7 million and has been recorded as goodwill, which is being amortized on a straight-line basis over 15 years.

Effective June 16, 1999, the Company purchased the assets of one of its franchisees for approximately $875,000. The acquisition was accounted for using the purchase method of accounting. The acquisition included two scoop shops located in Las Vegas, Nevada, and territory rights. The excess of the acquisition costs over the fair values of the net assets and liabilities acquired was $266,000 and has been recorded as goodwill, which is being amortized on a straight-line basis over ten years.

The assets acquired and liabilities assumed from the acquisitions included property, plant and equipment of approximately $1.2 million and long-term debt of approximately $1.9 million. These amounts, as well as current assets and liabilities of the acquired companies as of the acquisition dates, have been excluded from the consolidated statements of cash flows as non-cash items.

3.   SPECIAL CHARGE

In the fourth quarter of 1999, the Company recorded a special charge of $8.6 million dollars ($5.6 million after tax, or $0.78 per diluted share) in connection with the Company's plan to shift manufacturing of its frozen novelty line of business from a Company owned plant in Springfield, Vermont to third party co-packers to improve the Company's competitive position, gross margin and profitability. This action resulted in the fourth quarter 1999 write-off of assets associated with the ice cream novelty and other manufacturing assets and costs associated with severance for those employees who do not accept the Company's offer of relocation. This plan to shift novelty manufacturing will be executed during 2000. The outsourcing of its ice cream novelty business will

Notes to Consolidated Financial Statements
Dollars in tables in thousands except share data

enable the Company to introduce a wider range of novelty products in the future and increase its flexibility. The charge consists of certain one-time expenses, substantially all of which are non-cash. The special charge of $8.6 million consisted of $8.0 million for the write off or write down of fixed assets with the balance for employee severance.

4.   CASH AND INVESTMENTS

The following is a summary of cash, cash equivalents and investments as of December 25, 1999 and December 26, 1998:

	Cash and Cash Equivalents	December 25, 1999 Short-Term Investments	Investments
Cash	$10,762		
Commercial paper	198		
Tax exempt floating rate notes	900		
Municipal bonds	13,400	$11,474	
Preferred stock		9,094	
	25,260	20,568	
Certificates of deposit		763	$200
	$25,260	$21,331	$200

	Cash and Cash Equivalents	December 26, 1998 Short-Term Investments	Investments
Cash	$ 7,834		
Commercial paper	3,277		
Tax exempt floating rate notes	800		
Municipal bonds	13,200	$14,926	
Convertible bonds		955	
Preferred Stock		5,649	
	25,111	21,530	
Certificates of deposit		588	$303
	$25,111	$22,118	$303

The Company considers all of its investments, except for certificates of deposit, as available for sale. Certificates of deposit are held to maturity. Municipal bonds included in cash and cash equivalents mature at par in 30 to 45 days, at which time the interest rate is reset to the then market rate, and the Company may convert the investment to cash. Municipal bonds and convertible bonds recorded as short-term investments have varying maturities in 2000 and beyond, however, the Company does not intend to hold such investments to maturity. During 1999 and 1998, the Company also invested in fixed income preferred stock of primarily financial institutions.

Notes to Consolidated Financial Statements
Dollars in tables in thousands except share data

The Company determines the fair value of its short-term investments based on quoted market prices. Unrealized gains and losses on available for sale securities are excluded from earnings and are reported as a separate component of stockholders' equity until realized. At December 25, 1999, unrealized losses amounted to $324,000. At December 26, 1998, unrealized gains and losses on short-term investments were not significant.

Gross purchases and maturities aggregated $74.4 million and $77.9 million in 1999, $221.6 million and $228.4 million in 1998, and $43.1 million and $25.4 million in 1997. Realized gains and losses were not material for all periods presented.

5.   INVENTORIES

Inventories consist of the following:

	December 25, 1999	December 26, 1998
Ice cream and ingredients	$12,245	$12,025
Paper goods	659	524
Food, beverages and gift items	1,033	541
	$13,937	$13,090

6.   PROPERTY, PLANT AND EQUIPMENT

	Estimated Useful Lives/Lease Term	December 25, 1999	December 26, 1998
Land and improvements	15-25 years	$ 3,622	$ 4,520
Buildings	25 years	33,376	37,940
Equipment and furniture	3-20 years	48,517	52,047
Leasehold improvements	3-10 years	4,180	3,727
Construction in progress		4,265	2,058
		93,960	100,292
Less accumulated depreciation		37,403	36,841
		$ 56,557	$ 63,451

Depreciation expense for the years ended December 25, 1999, December 26, 1998 and December 27, 1997 was $8.8 million, $7.9 million and $7.4 million, respectively.

Notes to Consolidated Financial Statements
Dollars in tables in thousands except share data

7. ACCOUNTS PAYABLE AND ACCRUED EXPENSES

	December 25, 1999	December 26, 1998
Trade accounts payable	$10,079	$ 4,623
Accrued expenses	13,838	12,157
Accrued payroll and related costs	3,392	3,272
Accrued promotional costs	5,467	4,297
Accrued marketing costs	1,322	2,837
Accrued insurance expense	537	1,081
Income taxes payable	1,215	-
Deferred revenue	3,065	395
	$38,915	$28,662

8. LONG-TERM DEBT AND CAPITAL LEASE OBLIGATIONS

	December 25, 1999	December 26, 1998
Senior Notes - Series A payable in annual Installments beginning in 1998 through 2003 with interest payable semiannually at 5.9%	$13,357	$16,680
Senior Notes - Series B payable in annual installments beginning in 1998 through 2003 with interest payable semiannually at 5.73%	6,667	8,333
Other long-term obligations	2,272	744
	22,296	25,757
Less current portion	5,627	5,266
	$16,669	$20,491

Property, plant and equipment having a net book value of approximately $11.2 million at December 25, 1999 are pledged as collateral under certain long-term debt arrangements.

Long-term debt and capital lease obligations at December 25, 1999 maturing in each of the next five years and thereafter are as follows:

	Capital Lease Obligations	Long-term Debt
2000	$ 89	$ 5,561
2001	73	5,190
2002	21	6,047
2003	19	5,156
2004	16	62
Thereafter	184	--
Total minimum payments	402	22,016
Less amounts representing interest	122	--
	$280	$22,016

Notes to Consolidated Financial Statements
Dollars in tables in thousands except share data

The Company capitalized no interest in 1999, 1998 or 1997. Interest paid amounted to $1,698,000 $1,832,000 and $1,975,000 for 1999, 1998 and 1997, respectively.

The Company has available two $10,000,000 unsecured working capital line of credit agreements with two banks. Interest on borrowings under the agreements is set at the banks' base rate or at LIBOR plus a margin based on a pre-determined formula. No amounts were borrowed under these or any bank agreements during any of the years presented. The working capital line of credit agreements expire December 23, 2001.

Certain of the debt agreements contain restrictive covenants requiring maintenance of minimum levels of working capital, net worth, debt to capitalization ratios and earnings before interest, taxes, depreciation and amortization (EBITDA). Furthermore, distributions are limited to an amount of $5 million plus 75% of earnings and 100% of net losses since June 30, 1993; approximately $23.2 million of retained earnings at December 25, 1999 was available for payment of dividends. As of December 25, 1999, the Company received a waiver of compliance related to its working capital requirements.

As of December 25, 1999, the carrying amount and fair value of the Company's long-term debt were $22.3 million and $21.3 million, respectively, and as of December 26, 1998, they were $25.8 million and $24.4 million, respectively.

9.   STOCKHOLDERS' EQUITY

Preferred and Common Stock

The Class A Preferred Stock has one vote per share on all matters on which it is entitled to vote and is entitled to vote as a separate class in certain business combinations, such that approval of two-thirds of the class is required for such business combinations. The Class A Preferred Stock is redeemable by the Company, by the specified vote of the Continuing Directors (as defined in the Articles of Association). The Class A Common Stock has one vote per share on all matters on which it is entitled to vote. In June 1987, the Company's shareholders adopted an amendment to the Company's Articles of Association that authorized 3 million shares of a new Class B Common Stock and redesignated the Company's existing Common Stock as Class A Common Stock. The Class B Common Stock has ten votes per share on all matters on which it is entitled to vote, except as may be otherwise provided by law, may be converted into shares of Class A Common Stock by the specified vote of the continuing Directors is generally non-transferable as such and is convertible upon transfer into Class A Common Stock, on a one-for-one basis. A stockholder who does not wish to complete the prior conversion process may effect a sale by simply delivering the certificate for such shares of Class B Stock to a broker, properly endorsed. The broker may then present the certificate to the Company's Transfer Agent, which, if the transfer is otherwise in good order, will issue to the purchaser a certificate for the number of shares of Class A Common Stock thereby sold.

Accumulated Other Comprehensive Income (Loss)

Total comprehensive income amounted to $3.1 million for the year ended December 25, 1999 and $6.2 million and $3.9 million for the years ended December 26, 1998 and December 27, 1997, respectively. Other comprehensive income consisted of adjustments for net foreign currency translation gains (losses) in the amounts of $15,000, ($22,000) and ($11,000) for 1999, 1998 and 1997, respectively and unrealized losses on available for sale securities in the amount of $324,000

Notes to Consolidated Financial Statements
Dollars in tables in thousands except share data

beginning in 1999. The accumulated balance for foreign currency translation were $136,000, $151,000 and $129,000 for 1999, 1998 and 1997, respectively. Accumulated balances for unrealized losses on available for sale securities was $324,000 for the year ended December 25, 1999.

10. Shareholder Rights Plan

In August 1998, following approval by its Board of Directors, the Company put in place two Shareholder Rights Plans, one pertaining to the Class A Common Stock and one pertaining to the Class B Common Stock. These Plans are intended to protect stockholders by compelling someone seeking to acquire the Company to negotiate with the Company's Board of Directors in order to protect stockholders from unfair takeover tactics and to assist in the maximization of stockholder value. These Rights Plans, which are common for public companies in the United States, may also be deemed to be "anti-takeover" provisions in that the Board of Directors believes that these Plans will make it difficult for a third party to acquire control of the Company on terms which are unfair or unfavorable to the stockholders. Also, in April 1998, the Legislature of the State of Vermont amended a provision of the Vermont Business Corporation Act to provide that the directors of a Vermont corporation may also consider, in determining whether an acquisition offer or other matter is in the best interests of the corporation, the interests of the corporation's employees, suppliers, creditors and customers, the economy of the state in which the corporation is located and including the possibility that the best interests of the corporation may be served by the continued independence of the corporation.

11. STOCK BASED COMPENSATION PLANS

The Company has various stock option plans:

The 1995 and 1999 Equity Incentive Plans were established to provide grants to employees, and other key persons or entities, including non-employee directors who are in the position, in the opinion of the Compensation Committee, to make a significant contribution to the success of the Company, of incentive and non-incentive stock options, stock appreciation rights, restricted stock, unrestricted stock awards, deferred stock awards, cash or stock performance awards, loans or supplemental grants, or combinations thereof. While the Company grants options which may become exercisable at different times or within different periods, the Company has generally granted options to employees which vest over a period of four, five, or six years, and in some cases subject to acceleration of vesting upon specified events including a change in control (as defined). The exercise period cannot exceed ten years from the date of grant.

At December 25, 1999, 15,401 shares of Class A Common Stock were available for grant under the 1995 Equity Incentive Plan and 10,084 shares of Class A Common Stock were available for grant under the 1999 Equity Incentive Plan.

In addition, during 1999, the Company granted a total of 250,000 options to key employees under individual stock option agreements. The terms of these grants are similar to the terms of options granted under the 1995 Equity Incentive Plan.

The 1985 Option Plan provides for the grant of incentive and non-incentive stock options to employees or consultants. The 1985 Option Plan provides that options are granted with an exercise price equal to the market price of the Company's common stock on the date of grant. The 1985 Option Plan expired in August 1995, however, some options granted under this plan are outstanding as of December 25,

Notes to consolidated Financial Statements
Dollars in tables in thousands except share data

1999. While the Company grants options which may become exercisable at different times or within different periods, the Company has generally granted options to employees which vest over a period of four, five, or eight years, and in some cases with provisions for acceleration of vesting upon the occurrence of certain events. The exercise period cannot exceed ten years from the date of grant.

A summary of the Company's stock option activity and related information for the years ended December 25, 1999, December 26, 1998 and December 27, 1997 follows:

| | 1999 | | 1998 | | 1997 | |
	Options	Weighted Average Exercise Price	Options	Weighted Average Exercise Price	Options	Weighted Average Exercise Price
Outstanding at beginning of year	910,301	$12.97	910,811	$12.90	335,118	$14.49
Granted	616,396	22.60	42,500	17.79	694,000	12.04
Exercised	(131,376)	14.73	(36,629)	16.55	(80,000)	10.81
Forfeited	(91,771)	15.43	(6,381)	14.76	(38,307)	15.42
Outstanding at end of year	1,303,550	$17.18	910,301	$12.97	910,811	$12.90
Exercisable at end of year	561,243		382,021		203,552	
Available for future grants	25,485		284,220		345,893	

The following table presents weighted-average price and life information about significant option groups outstanding at December 25, 1999:

| | Options Outstanding | | | Options Exercisable | |
Range of Exercise Prices Price	Number Outstanding	Weighted Average Remaining Contractual Life	Weighted Average Exercise Price	Number Exercisable	Weighted Average Exercise
$10.63 –$10.88	370,000	6.96	$10.87	353,875	$10.87
12.38 – 16.75	302,834	6.77	13.92	191,837	14.29
19.00 – 19.25	26,500	5.82	19.01	15,531	19.01
21.00 – 28.06	604,216	9.39	22.60	0	0.00
$10.63 –$28.06	1,303,550	8.02	$17.18	561,243	$12.26

The Company maintains an Employee Stock Purchase Plan, which authorizes the issuance of up to 300,000 shares of common stock. All employees with six months of continuous service are eligible to participate in this plan. Participants in the plan are entitled to purchase Class A Common Stock during specified semi-annual periods through the accumulation of payroll deductions, at the lower of 85% of market value of the stock at the beginning or end of the offering period. At December 25, 1999, 152,016 shares had been issued under the plan and 147,984 were available for future issuance.

Notes to Consolidated Financial Statements
Dollars in tables in thousands except share data

The Company has a Restricted Stock Plan (the 1992 Plan) which provides that non-employee directors, on becoming eligible, may be awarded shares of Class A Common Stock by the Compensation Committee of the Board of Directors. Shares issued under the plan become vested over periods of up to five years. The Company has also adopted the 1995 Plan, which provides that non-employee directors can elect to receive stock in lieu of a Director's annual cash retainer. In 1999, 2,846 shares were issued to non-employee directors. These shares vest immediately. At December 25, 1999 a total of 15,105 shares had been awarded under these plans, all of which were fully vested, and 19,895 shares were available for future awards. Unearned compensation on unvested shares is recorded as of the award date and is amortized over the vesting period.

As of December 25, 1999, a total of 193,364 shares are reserved for future grant or issue under all of the Company's stock plans.

Pro forma information regarding net income and earnings per share is required by FAS 123, which also requires that the information be determined as if the Company has accounted for its employee stock options granted subsequent to December 31, 1994 under the fair value method of that Statement. The fair value for these options was estimated at the date of grant using a Black-Scholes option-pricing model with the following assumptions:

	1999	1998	1997
Risk-free interest rates	6.67%	5.10%	5.53%
Dividend yield	0.00%	0.00%	0.00%
Volatility factor	0.50	0.32	0.34
Weighted average expected lives (in years)	4.4	2.4	3.6

For purposes of pro forma disclosures, the estimated fair value of the options is amortized to expense over the options' vesting period. The impact on pro forma net income may not be representative of compensation expense in future years when the effect of the amortization of multiple awards would be reflected in the pro forma disclosures. The Company's pro forma information follows (in thousands except for earnings per share information):

	1999	1998	1997
Pro forma net income	$1,113	$5,935	$3,600
Pro forma earnings per share - diluted	$ 0.15	$ 0.80	$ 0.49
Weighted average fair value of options at the date of grant	$11.03	$ 4.22	$ 4.16

Notes to Consolidated Financial Statements
Dollars in tables in thousands except share data

12.   INCOME TAXES

The provision for income taxes consists of the following:

Federal	1999	1998	1997
Current	$4,082	$5,041	$ 3,300
Deferred	(2,443)	(2,093)	(1,388
	1,639	2,948	1,912
State			
Current	391	1,003	686
Deferred	(305)	(417)	(210)
	86	586	476
Foreign			
Current	24	-	-
Deferred	74	-	-
	98	-	-
	$1,823	$3,534	$2,388

Income taxes computed at the federal statutory rate differ from amounts provided as follows:

	1999	1998	1997
Tax at statutory rate	34.0 %	34.0 %	34.0 %
State tax, less federal tax effect	1.1	4.0	5.0
Income tax credits	0.0	(1.0)	(1.0)
Tax exempt interest	(8.7)	(3.0)	(2.9)
Valuation allowance	13.6	0.0	0.0
Foreign sales corporation	(8.3)	(1.0)	0.0
Other, net	3.3	3.1	2.9
Provision for income taxes	35.0 %	36.1 %	38.0 %

Notes to Consolidated Financial Statements
Dollars in tables in thousands except share data

Deferred income taxes reflect the net tax effects of temporary differences between the carrying amount of assets and liabilities for financial reporting purposes and the amounts used for income tax purposes and are attributable to the following:

	1999	1998
Deferred tax assets:		
Accrued liabilities	$4,383	$6,425
Inventories	1,651	1,413
Accounts receivable	434	430
Accrued special charge	1,779	-
Net operating losses	707	-
Other	-	475
	8,954	8,743
Valuation allowance	(707)	-
Total deferred tax assets	8,247	8,743
Deferred tax liabilities:		
Depreciation/property, plant and equipment	1,849	5,231
Other	351	139
Total deferred tax liabilities	2,200	5,370
Net deferred tax assets	$6,047	$3,373

The Company established a valuation allowance related to net operating loss carryforwards in certain foreign jurisdictions. Income taxes paid amounted to $2.2 million, $6.2 million and $2.2 million during 1999, 1998 and 1997, respectively.

13. EARNINGS PER SHARE

The following table sets forth the computation of basic and diluted earnings per share:

	1999	1998	1997
Numerator:			
Net income	$3,385	$6,242	$3,896
Denominator:			
Denominator for basic earnings per share - weighted-average shares	7,077	7,197	7,247
Dilutive stock options and warrants	328	266	87
Denominator for diluted earnings per share - adjusted weighted-average shares and assumed conversions	7,405	7,463	7,334
Net income per common share			
Basic	$ 0.48	$ 0.87	$ 0.54
Diluted	$ 0.46	$ 0.84	$ 0.53

Options to purchase 254,247 shares of common stock at prices ranging from $23.63 to $28.06 were outstanding during 1999 but were not included in the computation of diluted earnings per share because the options' exercise prices were greater than the average market price of the common shares and, therefore, the effect would be antidilutive. Options to purchase 32,500 shares of common stock at $19.25, and 146,811 shares of common stock at prices ranging from $16.75 to

Notes to Consolidated Financial Statements
Dollars in tables in thousands except share data

$19.00 were outstanding in 1998 and 1997, respectively, but were not included in the computation of diluted earnings per share because the options' exercise prices were greater than the average market price of the common shares and, therefore, the effect would be antidilutive.

Included in the computation of diluted earnings per share are warrants to acquire 125,000 shares, which are part of an agreement with an outside consultant. Under this agreement, when the average of the closing market value of the stock exceeds $22.00 per share over a 90 day period, the consultant would be entitled to purchase 125,000 shares of common stock at $14.00 per share. The 125,000 additional warrants became exercisable in March, 1999 and expire on July 1, 2004.

14. THE BEN & JERRY'S FOUNDATION, INC.

In October 1985, the Company issued 900 shares of Class A Preferred Stock to the Ben & Jerry's Foundation, Inc. (the Foundation), a not-for-profit corporation qualified under Section 501 (c)(3) of the Internal Revenue Code. The primary purpose of the Foundation is to be the principal recipient of cash contributions from the Company which are then donated to various community organizations and other charitable institutions. Contributions to the Foundation and directly to other charitable organizations, at the rate of approximately 7.5% of income before income taxes and special charges amounted to approximately $1,100,000, $793,000 and $510,000 for 1999, 1998 and 1997 respectively.

The Class A Preferred Stock is entitled to vote as a separate class in certain business combinations, such that approval of two-thirds of the class is required for such business combination. The three directors of the Foundation, including one of the founders of the Company, are members of the Board of Directors of the Company.

15. EMPLOYEE BENEFIT PLANS

The Company maintains profit sharing and savings plans for all eligible employees. The Company has also implemented a management incentive program, which provides for discretionary bonuses for management. Contributions to the profit sharing plan are allocated among all current full-time and regular part-time employees (other than the co-founders, Chief Executive Officer and Officers that are Senior Directors of functions) and are allocated fifty percent based upon length of service and fifty percent split evenly among all employees. The profit sharing plan and the management incentive plan are informal and discretionary. Recipients who participate in the management incentive program are not eligible to participate in the profit sharing plan. The savings plan is maintained in accordance with the provisions of Section 401(k) of the Internal Revenue Code and allows all employees with at least twelve months of service to make annual tax-deferred voluntary contributions up to fifteen percent of their salary. The Company contributes one percent of eligible employees' gross annual salary and may match the contribution up to an additional three percent of the employee's gross annual salary. Effective January 1, 1998, the Company amended its employees' retirement plan to permit contributions of shares of its stock to the plan from time to time. In 1998, the Board of Directors approved the contribution of $250,000 worth of Class A Common Stock to be allocated among all eligible employees' accounts. Total contributions by the Company to the profit sharing, management incentive program and savings plans were approximately $3.2 million, $2.7 million and $1.2 million for 1999, 1998 and 1997, respectively.

Notes to Consolidated Financial Statements
Dollars in tables in thousands except share data

16. COMMITMENTS

The Company leases certain property and equipment under operating leases. Minimum payments for operating leases having initial or remaining noncancellable terms in excess of one year are as follows:

2000	$1,402
2001	1,153
2002	940
2003	758
2004	417
Thereafter	383

Rent expense for operating leases amounted to approximately $1.6 million, $1.5 million and $1.2 million in 1999, 1998 and 1997, respectively.

17. SEGMENT INFORMATION

Ben & Jerry's Homemade, Inc. has one reportable segment: ice cream manufacturing and distribution. The Company manufactures super premium ice cream, frozen yogurt, sorbet and various ice cream novelty products. These products are distributed throughout the United States primarily through independent distributors and in certain foreign countries.

During 1999, 1998 and 1997 the Company's most significant customer, Dreyer's Grand Ice Cream, Inc. accounted for net sales of 40% in 1999 and 57% in 1998 and 1997. Sales and cash receipts are recorded and received primarily in U.S. dollars. Foreign currency exchange variations have little or no effect on the Company at this time. During 1999, the Company began doing business with Haagen-Dazs under a new distribution arrangement which accounted for 11% of net sales during the year.

Information concerning operations by geographic area are as follows:

	December 25, 1999	December 26, 1998	December 27, 1997
Sales to Unaffiliated Customers			
United States	$211,509	$191,777	$166,592
Foreign	25,534	17,426	7,614
	$237,043	$209,203	$174,206
Net Income (Loss)			
United States	$ 4,094	$ 6,444	$ 4,136
Foreign	(709)	(202)	(240)
	$ 3,385	$ 6,242	$ 3,896
Long-Lived Assets			
United States	$ 58,147	$ 64,722	$ 66,128
Foreign	5,108	2,470	263
	$ 63,255	$ 67,192	$ 66,391

Note: Foreign operations include the United Kingdom, France, Canada, The Netherlands, Belgium, Israel and Japan.

Notes to Consolidated Financial Statements
Dollars in tables in thousands except share data

18.   SELECTED QUARTERLY FINANCIAL INFORMATION (Unaudited)

	First Quarter1	Second Quarter1	Third Quarter1	Fourth Quarter1
1999				
Net sales	$50,066	$68,172	$67,129	$51,676
Gross profit	18,089	27,617	27,814	18,232
Net income (loss)	1,197	3,214	3,535	(4,561)2
Net income (loss) per common share				
Basic	.17	.45	.50	(.66)
Diluted	.16	.42	.47	(.66)
1998				
Net sales	$41,556	$58,749	$64,566	$44,332
Gross profit	13,964	21,153	24,227	13,634
Net income	380	2,130	2,892	840
Net income per common share				
Basic	.05	.29	.40	.12
Diluted	.05	.28	.39	.11

1   Each quarter represents a thirteen week period for all periods
     presented.

2   Fourth quarter reflects a non-recurring pre-tax special charge of
     $8,602 ($5.6 million after tax or $0.78 per diluted share). Net income,
     excluding the special charge was $1 million and diluted net income per
     common share was $0.14.